Mrs. Brown's FAMILY HANDBOOK

THE ULTIMATE GUIDE TO RUNNING YOUR HOME & FAMILY

Agnes Brown
with Brendan O'Carroll
and Michael Joseph

PENGUIN BOOKS

PENGUIN BOOKS

Published by the Penguin Group
Penguin Books Ltd, 80 Strand, London WC2R 0RL, England
Penguin Group (USA) Inc., 375 Hudson Street, New York, New York 10014, USA
Penguin Group (Canada), 90 Eglinton Avenue East, Suite 700, Toronto, Ontario, Canada
M4P 2Y3
(a division of Pearson Penguin Canada Inc.)
Penguin Ireland, 25 St Stephen's Green, Dublin 2, Ireland (a division of Penguin Books Ltd)
Penguin Group (Australia), 707 Collins Street, Melbourne, Victoria 3008, Australia
(a division of Pearson Australia Group Pty Ltd)
Penguin Books India Pvt Ltd, 11 Community Centre,
Panchsheel Park, New Delhi – 110 017, India
Penguin Group (NZ), 67 Apollo Drive, Rosedale, North Shore 0632, New Zealand
(a division of Pearson New Zealand Ltd)
Penguin Books (South Africa) (Pty) Ltd, Block D, Rosebank Office Park,
181 Jan Smuts Avenue, Parktown North, Gauteng 2193, South Africa

Penguin Books Ltd, Registered Offices: 80 Strand, London WC2R 0RL, England

www.penguin.com

First published by Michael Joseph 2013
Published in Penguin Books 2014
005

Text copyright © Brendan O'Carroll, Jason Hazeley and Joel Morris, 2013
Design copyright © Unreal Ltd, 2013
All photographs copyright © Bocpix Ltd, 2013
Additional images from Getty Images and Shutterstock
Photograph on p.278 of Sinéad O'Connor © Steve Granitz/Wire Image/Getty Images
The moral right of the copyright holders has been asserted

Printed in Great Britain by Clays Ltd, St Ives plc

ISBN: 978-1-405-91353-9

**This book
is dedicated to
all the feckin'
Mammys
of the world…**

Contents

I have to say I was intrigued when Daniel Bunyard approached me and suggested I put together a 'Family Handbook'. Intrigued for a few reasons. Firstly, I was flattered that he believed I could, in fact, do joined-up writing. Secondly, I'm just an ordinary mother, so I said to myself, *'Self... who would want to know what you have to say about getting a family through this busy and sometimes turbulent world?'*

And, finally, he was naked. That last one can be explained by the fact that I was standing in the sauna at Give it a Lash, our local gym – I was trying to get Rory to come home for his dinner.

My immediate reaction was, *'My God, straight pubic hair with a tinge of ginger – how interesting.'*

I gave his suggestion some thought over the next few minutes and realized that he had a good idea on his hands. I won't go into what I had in mine.

So here it is. Between the covers of this strange but riveting book are, I believe, everything you will need to know to survive any family event or occasion that arises. It does not go into the deeper subjects, like Global Warming, as that hasn't reached Ireland yet, nor is it meant to serve as a blueprint to a happy life. It's more of a handbook of how to cope with all the shit life throws at you. To date I have four grandsons, God's reward to me for not killing my kids. So there will probably be a follow-up book about being a Granny – I don't know yet.

Depending on where you look I have six or seven children. I know that is a rather large family by modern standards, but you have to remember there was no such thing as 'the pill' in my day, and because we had no access to condoms, protecting yourself against unwanted pregnancy meant improvising, and I should state here that cling film is not 100 per cent safe and tin foil is very uncomfortable. Iggy O'Brien, a neighbour of mine, was the first one to get the pill on our street. Her husband was a handyman in the local chemist shop and he 'acquired' some. As it turned out, what he'd actually got was Valium. So she was taking Valium for twenty years thinking they were birth control pills. Iggy has thirteen children, but she doesn't care.

One thing experience has taught me is that every child is different, especially Rory. I also learned that every birth is different; for instance, where Cathy was the picture of beauty when she was born, Dermot looked like a mini Winston Churchill. Don't even remind me about Rory's birth, he was a forceps job and he looked like I'd given birth to ET. But the births do get easier as they become more frequent. Mark, my eldest, had me in labour for 100 hours (they had to shave me twice) but Trevor, my youngest, just dropped out one night between the fourth and fifth races at the dogs.

I'll not go fully into the ins and outs of my own family in this introduction, sufficient to say that I would not swap one of them for all the tea in China. Each and every one of them has made me laugh, smile and wonder at how truly amazing life is. Oh, sure, from time to time they break your heart or drive you around the bend, but from the moment they were born each and every one of them became an addition to my life. I can't count the amount of times I stood over their beds, watching one or other of them asleep at the end of a busy day and thinking, *'I could kill that little bastard right now.'* Ha-ha!

No, seriously. If you are reading this and have young children, then cherish these years with them – every moment – because those years are fleeting and will never come again.

Right, that's that, I'm off to Magaluf for a couple of weeks with the money Ginger Balls has given me for this shite.

Mrs A. Brown

Mrs Agnes Brown
Dublin, Ireland

First things first . . .
Will you have a cup of tea?

Sure you will. Now, you might have read a lot of old crap about how to make the perfect cup of tea – there are scientists who've dedicated their lives to it, so you'd think, if you read the papers. Anyway, ignore all that shite. Here's the way to make tea, as passed down from Mammy to Mammy for countless generations. Just like the teapot should be. *(Your teapot might have 'Made in China' written underneath it. Mine's got a feckin' cave painting.)*

The perfect cup of tea

Right. Boiling water, tea, teapot. It's not feckin' rocket science. Anything more complicated is **NOT TEA**.

That's your feckin' equation for the perfect cup of tea.

Leaves or bags?

Makes no feckin' difference. What did you think was in those bags? Tea powder? Tea granules? Tea cubes? It's leaves. In a bag. And the bag's in a cup, or a pot. Simple. You're going to make a fuss about this, we're going to get nowhere, and valuable tea-drinking time is wasted.

Fancy-pants stuff that isn't real tea

Your supermarket shelves used to have about three types of tea: the one you liked, the one your friend liked, and the one no one liked. Life was easy.

Now there's hundreds of feckin' things on the tea aisle. Hundreds, I tell you. But they're not real teas. They're not even pretend teas. They're not tea. If it's tea, it'll have the word 'tea' on the box and no pictures. If it's not tea, it'll have a fancy photo and a long feckin' description that sounds like something that fell out of a book of poems. You don't need to describe tea. That's what the word 'tea' does.

Things that aren't tea:

⊘ Anything with a flower on the box

⊘ Anything with a name like 'peppermint infection'

⊘ Anything that's supposed to restore your balance *(Jaysus, you shouldn't be anywhere near boiling water if you can't stand up straight)*

⊘ Anything that sounds like it's off a Chinese takeaway menu

⊘ Anything that sounds like a medicine

⊘ Anything that grows next to the railway

⊘ Anything the same flavour as a toilet cleaner

⊘ Anything that rhymes *('A hint of mint' or 'Ginger binger')*

⊘ Anything that mentions a part of the body

⊘ Anything in a packet made of wallpaper

⊘ Anything that just tells you what colour it is

I've tried one of those things once. It was called 'Stomach Comfort' or something, and it tasted like tea without any tea. In other words, hot water. Which is all it feckin' was. I don't need to spend money on that. I've got the recipe for hot water at home.

Tea is tea. It's not flowers. Flowers are for flowerpots and tea is for teapots. You pour boiling water into your flowerpots, you might melt the plastic stems.

9

Your teapot

Don't clean it. There it is – it's that simple. All those years of caked-on tea add a richness to the flavour that can't be got from a new pot.

And means you can use fewer bags!

All you have to do is sluice some water round it once every forty years. Anything more is a waste of feckin' time.

My Auntie Niamh had this lovely old pot she called Brown Betty, a beautiful, shapely thing, with this deep mahogany colour. It was only when I got it in her will that I found out it was actually made of clear glass. That's a proper pot.

. . . .

The Teasmade

The robot Mammy. Redser always wanted one. I said no, because if you end up sharing your bed with a contraption that makes tea, you're at the top of a slippery slope. Next thing you'll be sharing your room with a machine that can perform another of your wifely duties. And no one wants a washing machine next to their pillow.

Besides, it's plain feckin' weird to think there's something making a cup of tea in your home while you're asleep. It's like having a very relaxed burglar.

Making them stay for a cuppa

Some people will find any old excuse not to hang around for a cup of tea. <u>Don't take any shite from them.</u> Try these:

EXCUSE	WHAT YOU SAY
I'm not thirsty	*Have a biscuit*
I don't drink tea	*How about one of my special coffees? (It's a tea)*
I'm allergic to caffeine	*But this is TEA*
I've got a plane to catch	*They charge you for tea on those – have a free one now*
I've got a doctor's appointment	*He might want a urine sample – fill your bladder*
I'm in a hurry	*It's already made, so*
I'm parked on a meter	*Those parking fines can be a hell of a shock – have a cup of tea*
I'd better get home – there's snow on the way	*A cup of tea will warm you up for the journey*
I'm off to a funeral	*It's what he would have wanted*
It's a bit late – I don't want to be awake all night	*I'll put one of the cat's pills in it – they make her fearful drowsy*
I just had one	*I know, but I can wash the cup up and give you another one*
I don't want to be any trouble	*Then you'll drink this cup of tea I've poured you*
Only if you're making yourself one	*Hello, I'm Mrs Brown – we've obviously never met*
I only drink fruit tea	*I'll put a spoonful of jam in it*
Just a glass of water, thanks	*Well, I've just boiled some water – I'll pop a bag in it and some milk – that'll help it cool down*
You've been up on your feet all day, – let me make you a cup of tea	*Grand idea – I'll show you how*
Nie pij herbat ('I don't drink tea')	*Nie mówi po polski – teraz pije herbat* *('And I don't speak Polish – now drink your tea')*
I'm nil by mouth	*I'll get one of the nurses to pour it into your bag*
I'm sorry, Mrs Brown, but he's dead	*What a terrible shock – I'll make EVERYONE a cup of tea*

TEA FACTS

MAMMY O'RIORDAN

MAMMY DUFF

MAMMY BRADY

STRONGEST EVER CUP OF TEA

*Mammy O'Riordan,
Cleggan Bay, 1972*

A bump on the head left Mammy O'Riordan with a terrible short memory – she forgot she'd put five bags in the pot before putting another five in. And another five. And this went on for some days, until she had 155 bags in the pot. Then she added the water and, God love her, forgot about that too. The other thing the bump on the head did was leave her with no sense of taste. So when she had a cup, she thought it was fine. But her poor husband Donny was hospitalized. To this day, they say you can still smell the tea in Cleggan Bay.

LONGEST DISTANCE A MAMMY HAS CARRIED A CUP OF TEA TO A GUEST

*Mammy Duff,
Ballyboghil, 1988*

Poor Mammy Duff made a cup of tea for Craig, her Aisling's husband, which he didn't drink before leaving for their flight back to Canada. Two years later, when Mammy Duff went over to see her new grandson, Jack, in Ontario, she came out of arrivals at the airport with her suitcase in one hand and Craig's cup of tea, still with the cling film over it, in the other. It had travelled 8,300km. And they say it was still warm. God knows where she kept it.

MOST CUPS OF TEA FROM ONE BAG

*Mammy Brady,
Dublin, 2010*

The recession hit Ireland hard, and what with Mammy Brady being a right feckin' skinflint as it was, wasn't it bound to happen that she'd start re-using her tea bags? When the local priest called round one morning, she gave him a cup of what looked like milky water. He asked her if he could just have a cup of tea. She said, 'That is tea. But in these times, Father, I can't be making just the one cup with every bag.' Turns out she'd been using the tea bag for three months. And that works out at about 1,500 cups of tea. The previous record holder was Mammy Doyle from Waterville, who got 350 cups out of the one bag after her local shop refused to serve her. (She'd stolen a cucumber and was trying to smuggle it out. Apparently it was the smile on her face that gave it away.)

MAMMY HOOLIHAN

GUMMY KIELY

MAMMY MURPHY

MOST CUPS OF TEA SERVED TO A DOOR-TO-DOOR SALESMAN

Mammy Hoolihan,
Nobber, 1969

The legendary Mammy Hoolihan was already well known for keeping an encyclopaedia salesman talking for 36 hours when she was called on by a man selling tea towels in July 1969. By the time he left, nearly a fortnight later, he'd had upwards of 200 cups of tea and man had landed on the moon. To celebrate this giant leap, Mammy Hoolihan bought a single cloth off him.

MOST SUGARS IN A CUP OF TEA

Gummy Kiely,
Knocktopher, 1995

Gummy was a right hard worker. Had been all his life. And he'd always liked his tea fierce sweet. So sweet that, by the time he was in his mid-forties, he'd lost all his teeth. Gummy said that meant the gloves were off, and started having sweeter and sweeter tea. At his retirement in 1995, the factory boss – who Gummy had never met before – invited him off the floor and up into his posh office to give him a tie and a feckin' clock. Gummy was offered a cup of tea. 'Thank you,' he said, 'Forty-three sugars please.' They never did get the residue off the cup.

QUICKEST OFFER OF A CUP OF TEA

Mammy Murphy,
Donegal, various
1964 present

Mammy Murphy prides herself on being the fastest tea-server in the whole of Ireland. She was always known for coming to the door with a cup of tea, but then she got quicker, and started running down the path to offer callers a cup of tea before they'd even got the gate open. She's even faster than that now. Couple of years ago she had a plumber round. She was his last call of the day, due around 4 p.m. But that morning, when he left the depot at 7 a.m., there was a cup of tea sitting on the passenger seat of his van. There are feckin' members of the Magic Circle could learn a thing or two from Mammy Murphy.

COASTERS

Coasters are all that stand between your polished surfaces and wet ring marks. I can't think of anything feckin' worse than wet ring marks, and I can think of herpes. Ugh. But no. Wet ring marks are worse. Now, coasters can cost a feckin' fortune in the shops. But here's one you can cut out and use for nothing!

 ⟶ ⟶

The design is all my own, and Dermot reckons it could be a big seller if I mass-produce them. Like that 'Keep Calm and Carry On' thing, but more popular.

Anyway, I'm giving it away here. Don't say I never give you anything.

Just buy twenty or so copies of this book and you'll have enough coasters to cater for any occasion! A rugby club could come for a piss-up in your front room without anyone leaving a wet mark! Apart from Winnie on the sofa. I think it's the shorts that get her going.

INSTRUCTIONS

1. Get some scissors. Not the best scissors, I don't want to blunt them, for feck's sake. What if I wanted to make a dress? No, I'm not planning on making a feckin' dress. But what if I was? Just put them back and get the not-best ones out of the drawer by the sink with all the shite in it. I know they're blunt, but that's safer. You don't want to go cutting something. Feck off.

2. Cut out round the coaster where indicated. That's the dotted line, in case you've never seen the back of a cornflakes packet before.

3. Paste the coaster to something stiff, like Dermot's sheets after he's been thumbing through his dirty magazines. Or you could paste my coaster to something the same size and shape, but thicker. Like a coaster, for instance. Buy some from a shop. They're not that expensive, for feck's sake.

And, hey presto! Your surfaces are safe! No more mug rings on your prize walnut. Mammy does it again.

TEA TOWELS

You might think a tea towel is just a tea towel. But you'd be a feckin' idiot if you did.

It is your tool.

You don't want to be caught with the wrong tool in your hand. Or sure there could be a terrible mess. And if you find yourself with a terrible mess on your hands, what do you need?

That's right. A tea towel.

The tea towel is a Mammy's weapon of choice.

Robin Hood had his bow and arrow. King Arthur had his Excalibur in the stone. Your lad Skywalker from that film had that kitchen strip-light, and mighty thankful he was for it when he was scrapping with your man with the bucket on his head and the Woodbine cough.

And a Mammy has her **Best Tea Towel.**

Never mix up your Best Tea Towel with the Not-Best Tea Towels. As it probably says in the Bible, 'By your tea towels shall your daughter's mother know ye when she starts poking round your kitchen like a feckin' bloodhound.'

You don't want her seeing your second- or third-best tea towel, and giving you that look that says, 'Last time I stumbled upon something that filthy in my house, I made my hubby pay for it on the cable bill out of his own feckin' money.'

The Best Tea Towel is worn over the shoulder. It's your mark of office as a Mammy, your stripes of command, showing you're ready for action, whatever gets spilled, whatever goes wrong, whoever needs a feckin' good clout round the ear to mind their feckin' language.

The Mammy, shown here in full dress uniform.

A CHART OF TEA TOWELS

Grade One:
BEST

THICKNESS: Hold it up to the kitchen window. Light can't pass through it.

COLOUR: Bright as the day you bought it.

DESIGN: Souvenir of major national occasion or place of interest ('Gay Byrne: 90 Years in Showbusiness', 'Limerick Tureen Museum', 'Sligo House of Wool')

WHERE? Public display. Hanging over oven door. Stuffed carefully in one of those plastic holders like a cat's arse. Over the shoulder.

Grade Two: B
SECOND BEST

THICKNESS: Hold it up to the kitchen window. Light can pass through it.

COLOUR: Faded. Like a flash photo of the Turin feckin' Shroud.

DESIGN: Souvenir of minor national occasion or place of interest ('Jedward: Two Years in Showbusiness', 'Wicklow Jedwardrome', 'Rathangan Jedward Monument')

WHERE? In a drawer, for family eyes only.

Grade Three: RESERVE

★★☆☆☆

THICKNESS: Hold it up to the kitchen window. A feckin' bluebottle can pass through it.

COLOUR: The summer skies of County Kerry (charcoal).

DESIGN: Feck knows. Incontinence kilt?

WHERE? Back of drawer with keys, pre-Eurozone coins, plastic bits of shite.

Grade Four: THE FAMILY DISGRACE

☆☆☆☆☆

THICKNESS: Hold it up to the kitchen window. Neighbours complain.

COLOUR: Shipwreck grey.

DESIGN: Your late father's pants. It'd be a wicked shame to let them go to waste.

WHERE? Cleaning cupboard, dog basket, toolshed, wrapped round child's hamster before burial in garden.

TEA TOWEL DISCIPLINE IS A TEST OF A MAMMY'S LIGHTNING REFLEXES.

You see some idiot about to mop the dog down with one of the best tea towels, you'll be moving like Usain feckin' Bolt with his arse on fire. Best tea towels are the only ones you'll be pegging out on the line for the neighbours to see. Anything below grade two goes straight to the back of the hot press where it can dry in shame. Standards. Standards. You don't get undressed in the feckin' window. Unless you're Kitty Sweeney and you'll do anything for feckin' attention, even if it's the police. *Dirty cow.*

SELF-DEFENCE

Tea towel self-defence is one of those martial arts, like Kung Fu and Chop Suey, handed down from Mammy to daughter over the generations. If you've your tea towel at the ready, and you know your moves, you can fend off anything from an insect to a pair of bailiffs. So keep your tea towel clean, folded and in position. A Mammy has to be ready for anything. She's like a coiled spring. But with less chance of needing a doctor's freezing cold hands to remove the feckin' thing.

 Attack

The basic attack is
The Wallop.

 1.
Keep the tea towel cocked *(that's folded up, before you start with your filthy talk)* and ready on the left shoulder.

2.
Grab the tea towel firmly with the right hand.

 3.
In one move, whip the tea towel off the shoulder and up into the air, bringing it down with a sharp backhand on whatever fecker is annoying you: fly, dog, sex pest, family member or all of the above – in other words, Grandad.

4.
If one Wallop isn't enough, don't hang about – lift the tea towel away in the other direction and bring it down forehand for a second whacking.

 5.
If two Wallops aren't enough *(and sometimes with Grandad it can take a dozen or so before the old fecker gets the message)*, repeat from the backhand again. Keep a steady one-two rhythm, and make as much noise as you can.

Attack

The second sort of attack is
The Sideswipe.

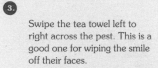

1. We'll take the cocking
as read.

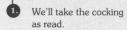

2. Grab the tea towel firmly with the right hand.

3.

Swipe the tea towel left to
right across the pest. This is a
good one for wiping the smile
off their faces.

4. Swipe again, right to left.

5. Repeat as necessary, making
a right racket the while.

Attack

For a proper sharp shot, you need a precision attack like **The Ping**.

1. Lift the tea towel slowly from the shoulder with both hands, one at each end.

2. Pull the tea towel tight, keeping it stretched. The tighter you pull it, the bigger the attack.

3. Release the towel from the back hand **while flicking it as hard as your poor wrists'll let you with the other hand**. It should feel like a feckin' catapult just went off in your hands.

4. Clean the squashed wasp off the towel and scrape its little guts off the cake. Unless it's Hilary's slice. God knows she already looks like she's chewing one.

Defence

You'll find that just wielding your tea towel in one hand is usually enough to keep the feckers at a distance. But you might need the odd manoeuvre.

A. This is the Don't You Come At Me With That Thing.

B. Here's the Knuckle Duster. Good for delivering a non-lethal thump.

(Translation: A Mammy has to be ready for anything)

C.

And here's the Bullfighter.

Shame there isn't a **bullshitfighter, really. Mind you, I'd never get anything** done if I had to constantly fend off the amount of rubbish I hear.

Cleaning

You don't run a family home for as long as I feckin' have without picking up a few things. Mainly socks.

Cleaning and picking up. Washing and scrubbing. Ah, the Mammy's lot.

Married life is meant to be romantic, but it's hardly Mills and feckin' Boon. It's more like *Brief Encounter*, with the number of briefs you encounter and peg out with the rest of the feckin' washing, day after feckin' day. Jaysus. I've handled more damp Y-fronts than a canalside brasser.

But I say housework can be romantic.

A clean house – that is the cornerstone of a woman's pride. It may sound old-fashioned, but a clean home shows you care

for your kids, you care for your man, and you care for yourself. And in my book – *and this is my feckin' book* – there's nothing more romantic than that.

I remember on our wedding night, Redser looked me in the eyes and whispered, 'Are you really my wife?'

'Yes,' I breathed.

'And you're prepared to perform all the duties of a wife?'

'Yes,' I said, bracing myself against the headboard.

'Then pick those up and pop them in the laundry basket, would you?'

Bone feckin' idle, he was.

Stains & Marks

There are a few old tricks worth remembering.

Alcohol

CLEANING TRICK
No.1

You can get anything off with alcohol. Ink. Coffee. Knickers.

A red wine stain is easily got rid of with white wine, unless you've already drunk all the white wine and that's why you spilled the red wine.

HANDY STAIN CHART

STAIN	CAN BE REMOVED WITH
RED WINE	WHITE WINE
WHITE WINE	WASHING-UP LIQUID
WASHING UP LIQUID	WATER
WATERMARKS	ALCOHOL

Jaysus. It's like singing feckin' 'Michael Finnegan'. Knock over a glass of Aldi plonk and you'd never leave the bucking house again.

Actually, it's not just wine. You can easily deal with problem stains using any alcohol. You just have to drink enough of the stuff to not give a feck about the stain.

The best way to avoid wine stains is not to spill any wine. Dr Flynn never spills a drop. You could pour him a glass, strap him into one of those feckin' things they train astronauts in, and he'd not lose a splash. Show me a spotless carpet and I'll show you a tightfisted alcoholic.

Alcohol. Proven to remove...

☑ Coffee   ☑ Ink   ☑ Knickers

Bread

**Bread is the staff of
life, the food our Lord
offered to his disciples
in remembrance of Him.**
It's also the absolute bollocks
for getting marks off walls,
especially if you've bumped
the paintwork with furniture
or a family member's head.

> **Keeping your blinds clean will increase their life, and that'll save a fortune. Blinds are so expensive these days, I saw a fellow down the shops shaking a tin trying to raise money for some. Cheeky fecker.**

I found that handy tip snipped out on the back of some magazine coupons for meat squares that had expired (The coupons. Not the squares.) I get a lot of my household tips that way.

Bread is also useful for bringing the sparkle back to something or other. I don't feckin' know. Furniture? Teeth? Marriage? I'd cashed in that part of the coupon against some knockdown tinned pork before I turned it over and read the back. Your guess is as feckin' good as mine.

Handy Tip

An L-shaped crust is great for taking dust off Venetian blinds. Just run it the length of the blind, and presto, the dirt is gone! Mind you, your bread is feckin' filthy. Still, no one'll notice once it's toasted.

Bargain Meatz

EX

LIMIT ONE PLEASE

Hormel

Chicken Breast

30c with this coupon

CLU#987

Terms and Conditions:
1 coupon per customer, per offer, per day. Cannot be used with any other offer. Offer ends 05/08/2009. Void if photocopied or altered.

How to get stains off your bread

CLEANING INSTRUCTIONS

BROWN BREAD — 40°   WHITE BREAD — 90°

You feckin' idiot. You've ruined some perfectly good bread. Sure, a bit of dirt's good for kids, toughens them up, but kids that'll turn their noses up at marmalade with bits in will go off the feckin' edge if their sandwiches are dirtier than a navvy's hanky.

How to clean your bread, then? Simple. Pop it in the washing machine at 40 degrees. Or if it's white bread, 90 degrees. Dry it off by laying it on top of a second-best tea towel in the back of the hot press. Or stick it under Grandad for five minutes after he's had pea soup. (Mind you, it might get stained again that way if he follows through. He's like one of those squids that pisses ink sometimes.)

Stains & Marks

Vinegar

CLEANING TRICK
No.3

There was a thing on the box about this la-di-da stately home, and the toffee-nosed housekeeper was cleaning every other thing with vinegar.

Feckin' vinegar?

The silver. The furniture. The bucking carpets. The place had more vinegar in it than a pickled egg. And I thought, **Jaysus, can't you stretch to some feckin' Pledge?**

It doesn't matter if you're living in Downton feckin' Abbey – if the whole place smells like O'Houlihan's Fish Bar, people are going to think you're common as muck.

By the way, if your home does smell like O'Houlihan's Fish Bar, here are two simple tips.

1. Spray some feckin' Pledge about.

2. Lock the door to stop Dermot bringing Buster back bevvied to the skies, with a feckin' bag of one-and-one from the chippy and leaving it down the back of the telly, all stinking of haddock worse than a dockside bin. Jaysus. Is it any wonder Grandad's got mice?

O'Houlihan's
FISH BAR

Methylated Spirits

CLEANING TRICK
No.4

Methylated spirits are good to clean stuff, apparently. I wouldn't know. The bottle's always feckin' empty, Grandad.

Laundry

They say the invention of the washing machine revolutionized the lives of women. Too feckin' right. I can't believe I used to just stand by and watch the fecker go round. That's called looking a gift horse in the mouth, that is.

I've had a more fulfilling sexual relationship with my Zanussi than I ever did with Redser, God rest his soul. I swear, if I'd known about this forty years ago, and could have fitted it into me dad's old suit, I'd have married the feckin' thing.

I heard about this from one of Cathy's magazines. *Break A Leg*, or something. They make them handbag-sized now, you know, which is where I came across it, accidentally going through her handbag, and I tell you it wasn't the only thing I came across that day.

But you need to know what you're doing. Here's a useful guide to washing machine settings. You can even put some washing in, if you feel like it. Kill two birds with one stone.

MAMMY'S TIP

Lock the door and close the curtains in case anyone drops by. And stuff a Best Tea Towel in your mouth, for God's sake. I had Winnie hammering on the windows and calling the police thinking I was being murdered in my own feckin' kitchen.

Setting 9
Perfect length if he wants to watch the football.

Off

Setting 1
For heavily soiled whites.

Setting 8
Perfect for a quick one.

Setting 2
Long enough to bring in the telly.

Setting 7
Filthy.

Setting 3
Like you're on a mechanical bull.

Setting 6
Feckin' useless.

Setting 4
Surprisingly satisfying with a strong finish.

Setting 5
Firm enough to get a result.

USER GUIDE

SETTING 1
COTTON / HEAVILY SOILED WHITES
Temperature: 90 DEGREES
Max speed: 1100 RPM
Ride duration: 145 minutes

Result: Heavily soiled whites? You're feckin' telling me. I've ruined several pairs of perfectly good undercrackers on this setting.

SETTING 2
COTTON / SOILED WHITES, RESISTANT COLOURS
Temperature: 60 DEGREES
Max speed: 1100 RPM
Ride duration: 120 minutes

Result: A 'bluey whites' wash. That is, long enough to bring in the little telly and watch a blue film while you're riding, if that's your thing. Prevert.

SETTING 3
COLOURED COTTON / LIGHT SOILING
Temperature: 40 DEGREES
Max speed: 1100 RPM
Duration: 100 minutes

Result: Enough to have you slapping the work surfaces and thrashing about like you're on one of those mechanical bulls they have down Foley's on Rodeo Night. Clear best china from the drying rack before climbing aboard.

SETTING 4
SYNTHETICS / HEAVY SOILING, RESISTANT COLOURS
Temperature: 50 DEGREES
Max speed: 800 RPM
Duration: 80 minutes

Result: Surprisingly satisfying with a strong finish. I nearly fell off after half an hour because I couldn't make a fist to grip the edge of the machine. I was going to get our Mark to fit some handles to it, but he'd only have asked questions.

SETTING 5
WOOL, CASHMERE
Temperature: 40 DEGREES
Max speed: 600 RPM
Duration: 55 minutes

Result: Fair enough. Firm enough to get a result, but gentle enough not to wake babies or crack floor tiles.

SETTING 6
SILK / CURTAINS
Temperature: 30 DEGREES
Max speed: 0 RPM
Duration: 50 minutes

Result: 0 RPM? Feckin' useless. You might as well squat on the upstairs seat of a broken-down bus.

SETTING 7
JEANS / DENIM
Temperature: 40 DEGREES
Max speed: 800 RPM
Duration: 70 minutes

Result: Full head-back action with bells and whistles. Filthy. You know that scene in *When Dirty Harry Met Sally?* 'I'll have what she's having, punk'? Made my feckin' day, I can tell you.

SETTING 8
EXPRESS WASH / REFRESH
LIGHTLY SOILED GARMENTS
Temperature: 30 DEGREES
Max speed: 800 RPM
Duration: 15 minutes

Result: Perfect for tucking in a quick one. For example, while Grandad's having forty winks, or if you've popped to the kitchen and someone's asked for their tea strong.

SETTING 9
SPORTS WASH
Temperature: 30 DEGREES
Max speed: 600 RPM
Duration: 90 minutes

Result: Perfect length for if he wants to watch the football. 'I'm off to do my whites' and no questions asked. Back of the bucking net!

CLEANING YOUR WASHING MACHINE

Cleaning the washing machine is essential. Give the top a wipe over at least, for feck's sake. You don't want people to think you've got an invasion of snails.

FACT
The average family produces two tonnes of washing a year. Then they bring it round to their Mammy because she's got a feckin' drier.

THE WASHING LINE

Your washing line is a public place, remember. People judge you by it.

When Maureen Conway put out her split-crotch Donald Duck outfit, she couldn't show her face for months. She had to do her shopping in the dark. And it's all end-of-the-day reductions by then. God knows how she managed on stale bread and miniature yoghurts. It's no wonder she got a yeast infection.

Nothing shames a washing line worse than telltale stains. And I'm not talking about egg and Ribena – I mean the bad stuff. The downstairs department. The old ginger stripe. My advice is, if you've got a Grandad who's prone to a bit of smudging, buy him plenty of pairs of tiger-pattern pants. You can get away with murder with those on your line.

CARPETS & FLOORS

Carpets can take a fierce beating from a growing family. Keep them regularly hoovered (the carpets, not the growing family) and there's half the work done. But you're going to get marks and stains, whatever you do. It only takes one good wake and the floor can end up looking like a join-the-dots puzzle.

You can use this to your advantage. Wait until the stains join up. Hey presto – a whole new colour of carpet. This is why it's important to stick to a regular tipple. The same sort of cider makes the same colour of spot. You start mixing your drinks, and your carpet will end up looking like you've flayed a load of tortoiseshell cats.

CIGARETTE BURNS

Move a piece of furniture to cover the mark. Or buy a piece of furniture to cover it. Peggy Conroy's house is like a feckin' assault course. No one needs fourteen occasional tables. There aren't that many occasions.

Put a spare bangle round the fag burn and say it's a built-in ashtray. If they're drunk enough, they'll believe you. And by then, it's too late for the poor carpet anyway.

Or use a good shop-bought spot remover. Like Clearasil.

Fifty Shades
of Grey Pants

Colour of knickers	What to do
GRANDAD'S HAIR	90° wash, plenty of bicarb. (Applies to Grandad's hairwash too)
BUTTON MUSHROOM	Boil the hell out of them
CORPSE	Add some Tipp-Ex to your wash
BREEZE BLOCK	Hang it between two dark things on your line
BATTLESHIP	Say you cut them out of a boiler suit
PAVEMENT	Stick them in the jumble – someone'll have them for dusters
COALMINER'S BATHWATER	Dye them purple and keep them for special occasions
NEWSPRINT	Give up, for feck's sake

You buy it white, stick it in a whites wash, and it comes out grey. Feck knows the boffins must have been sagging off school the day they did keeping whites white. You can sometimes recover the dazzle to your vajazzlebags, though. Depends on how far along the scale they are.

Of course, the other thing you can do is re-christen them. Like they do with paints. Sure, you can't buy a grey paint now – I've seen Mark's colour swatches – they're all exotic names like 'Intense Truffle' and 'Graphite'. So, if any nosy bugger asks what's happened to your whites, tell them they're not white, they're posh. ***Then give them one of these silly feckin' names:***

Brushed Aluminium

Valley Slate

Dawn Concrete

Mellow Tyremark

Misty Phlegm

Mountaineer's Porridge

Drainpipe Blush

Overcast Oyster

Municipal Car Park

Dusted Slug

Robot Sunset

Muted Pensioner

Shane MacGowan's Toothbrush

Exotic Hooverbag

Luxury Donkey

TEENAGER STAINS

I don't think I want to go up this particular hill. I know, I know, it's natural for them to . . . you know . . . tickle the trunk . . . but the less said about that, the better. Sure I remember catching Dermot under his duvet with a Freemans catalogue. He said he was looking for a new hat. I said, there's cheaper ways of getting a hat than cutting one of them fancy bras in half.

And the filth you find under their beds. I've pulled out socks that are so stiff you could hammer fence posts into place with them.

MAMMY'S TIP Always wear gloves and a mask before starting on a teenager's room. Treat it like a meltdown at a nuclear power station. In both cases, you can bet there's an overheating rod to blame.

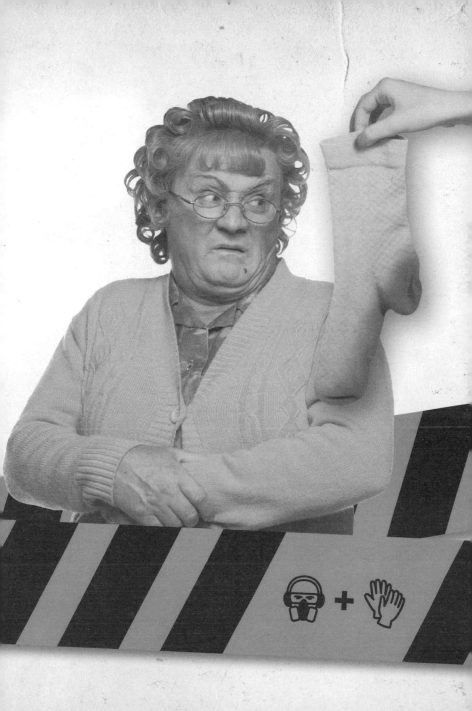

WASHING UP

Washing-up always feels like practice to me. Like one day I'm going to get good enough to get through to the washing-up final and go head-to-head with some puffed-up mannequin from Sandymount in her bright pink Marigolds. God knows, I'm good enough at it by now. I can clean up after a whole Sunday roast before Grandad's cleared his plate. Sometimes I can even wash his cutlery between mouthfuls.

WASHING-UP GLOVES

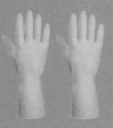

Mrs Marigold's twins

No matter what you do, you will always find two right-handed washing-up gloves from mismatched pairs under the sink. They find each other, like feckin' homing pigeons. And you end up with a left hand in a right-hand glove, with your poor thumb crammed into something the size of a pinkie. Three plates' worth of washing-up later, you've got thumbs like a bloated Fonz.

DRYING-UP

Blender blade / Ninja Star

Most of your cleaned stuff will do very nicely on the drying-up rack. There's an art to stacking it: small dainty stuff at the bottom, great big feckin' pans on the top. Like a woman's figure. Anything weird, like the bits of a blender, have to be dried up straight away. And you'll get a lot of marks in Mammy's book if you can ever – and I mean ever – get all the bits of a blender dry without grating your fingers to feckin' shreds. Whose brilliant idea was it to put lethal blades at the bottom of a great big glass jug you can barely get your arm into? You wouldn't put a mousetrap in a feckin' tombola, would you?

DISHWASHERS

Like a second wife

What are they bucking good for? They're like a second wife. I'm not having a robot upstaging me in my house. Scarlet bloody woman. Mind you, they're a cracking way to bake porridge on to a bowl. Porridge is the hardest feckin' substance known to man. They should cover tanks in it.

If you can't afford a dishwasher, you can do like Dermot did when he first moved out of home – hide the washing-up in any old cupboard and forget about it. Just like a dishwasher, really, and with half the plumbing.

HOOVERING

CONTENTS

Changing a hoover bag

The best hoover attachments
for cleaning Grandad

How to remove hoover
attachments from Grandad

CHANGING A HOOVER BAG

This may come as a surprise to the likes of Dermot but you can change a hoover bag. To be honest, it might come as a surprise to Dermot that you can feckin' hoover. I think he thinks the fairies do it.

HERE'S HOW TO CHANGE A HOOVER BAG:

No wisecracks about Rory and Dino please.

- Lift the lid on the hoover
- Put it back and hoover up the mess
- Remove the bag
- Put the bag back and hoover up the mess
- Remove the bag again and put it in the bin
- Hoover up the mess
- Realize you've forgotten to put a new bag in your hoover
- Borrow another hoover
- Lift the lid on your hoover
- Hoover out the inside of your hoover with the borrowed hoover
- Put a new bag in your hoover

Then repeat, to empty the bag of the hoover you borrowed.

> *The measure of a Mammy is how she cleans into tricky corners. The gap down the side of the dresser. Between the stair rods. The cleft under Grandad's chin.*

THE BEST HOOVER ATTACHMENTS FOR CLEANING GRANDAD

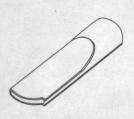

THE POINTY ONE

Good for behind the ears, between the fingers, under the you-know-what.

TOP TIP: Put a piece of hanky over the end before attaching the nozzle, and you can empty his pockets of small change and nip off down the bingo.

THE POKY BRUSH

Good for removing dog hair from Grandad, and Grandad hair from the dog. Can become so clogged it looks like a cuddly toy, and can be used as an emergency Christmas gift for an unliked neighbour's grandchild.

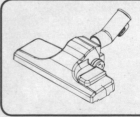

THE COMBINE HARVESTER

Crude but efficient. Cleans Grandad in one sweep but risks waking him up.

Once you've cleaned Grandad, put the hoover away. More times than I care to remember, I've been called away from my hoovering to answer the door to one of them Jehoover's Witnesses, and come back to discover Grandad doing something unspeakable to one of the attachments. Any port in a feckin' storm.

HOW TO REMOVE HOOVER ATTACHMENTS FROM GRANDAD

! **IMPORTANT:** UNPLUG THE FECKIN' HOOVER BEFORE YOU DO ANY OF THIS. He's already worked up. You don't want to make matters worse by suddenly hitting the on switch.

THE POINTY ONE

Work it loose from whichever fold or hole it's gone in. If that's too tough, try sprinkling a bit of dust under his nose. A good sneeze usually opens his hatches.

THE POKY BRUSH

I call this move the Jesse Owens, because it's a quick yank. A short, sharp execution – just grab it, take a deep breath and whip it off. Take any longer than that, and you're likely to make the problem worse. The more you fiddle, the bigger the widdle.

THE COMBINE HARVESTER

Sure, I've seen some things in my time, but I've never seen one of these get stuck to Grandad. There's nothing on the human body that shape. Not unless your cosmetic surgeon had a rotten fit of the shakes.

MAMMY'S TIP
You don't need a hoover if your dog's got worms. Just stick a tea towel to its arse and it'll do the floor in half the time.

RECYCLING AND RUBBISH

One thing that comes out of any family is a whole lot of rubbish. In my house, it's mainly packaging, food scraps and everything Buster says.

Rubbish

**Food in the dog.
Everything else in the bin.**

And what goes on in the
bathroom stays in the
bathroom. If I'm unlucky.
And then I have to unblock
the feckin' thing.

Food   Everything else

—— _Fig. 1_ ——

Recycling

Get to feck. Washing your
rubbish? It's a short step from
that to walking on toilet paper
like that Howard Huge.

Mad   Mad

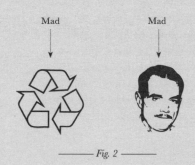

—— _Fig. 2_ ——

Mammy's Tip

**Gift-wrap your rubbish
and leave it on the doorstep.
Someone will take it away.**

Step 1   Step 2

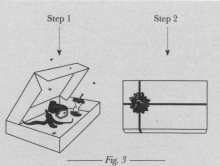

—— _Fig. 3_ ——

ROOM BY ROOM

Making a house a home isn't easy. In every room, you have to stay on top of things, or you'll go under (except the bedroom, where I find going under is less strain on your back). So let's walk through each room in turn, and hopefully by the time you get to the cream carpet on the landing, you'll have walked that feckin' dogshit off your shoes.

THE HALL

The first thing people see of your home (unless Dermot's dropped his keys down the pub and fallen asleep on the doorstep) is the hallway. It's not a room, more of a corridor – but it needs a Mammy's touch.

THE WELCOME MAT

I remember when my lot were on the verge of adulthood, I brought the welcome mat in off the doorstep and put it inside the hall, so they might think that that big old outside world was welcoming them with open arms and a cup of tea. Anything to tempt them to feckin' leave.

Welcome mats come in all shapes and sizes, but they're mainly rectangular and the width of a door. And a lot of them have funny messages on like **'Hello, I'm Mat'** and **'Beware of the Mat'**. Not my cup of tea, but each to his own, so. If I had a novelty mat, it'd say something like:

Hello there, Father

POST-OP
COCONUT

NO MORE THAN
TWO FEET AT A TIME

— I'VE SEEN —
BETTER SHOES
IN A KNACKER'S YARD

IS THAT A SMILE
OR DID YOU FORGET
your pants?

LOOK WHAT THEY DID
TO THEIR DOG

YOU TREAT ME LIKE
A DOORMAT

Get off me
YOU'RE RUINING MY HAIR

FUCK OFF,
HILARY

THE SHOE RACK

Your shoe rack says a lot about you. A rack full of shoes means you're popular or the family have dropped round yet again because you're such a great Mammy, or maybe you've enough money to have lots of shoes, like your mad woman from the Philippines, Impala Marcos.

An empty shoe rack says the opposite: you're unpopular, there's nobody visiting, and you can't afford shoes because you wasted the money on a shoe rack that doesn't get feckin' used.

One way to look popular or busy is to pop down the shoe bins. They're normally emptied on a Friday, so if you get down there Thursday night, they've slightly overflowed and you can pick up some unwanted shoes to use as props.

Just don't forget to choose shoes that look plausible. Poor Ginny Doyle was questioned by the police for three hours when someone spotted a pair of Peppa Pig wellies in her shoe rack. She never had kids. Just cats.

THE SMOKE ALARM

You can't be doing without one of these in a family home. Otherwise how are you going to know you're cooking bacon?

The fellow who invented these gadgets knew the biggest danger in the home was falling asleep while making sausages. There's no chance of that happening with this thing going off like a feckin' air-raid siren every time you brown toast.

A skilled Mammy, with a sturdy Best Tea Towel, can flick cooking smells away from a smoke detector with one hand while turning the bacon with the other. It's like feckin' ballet. I challenge Bruce Lee to get past when I'm grilling a chop.

Mammy's Tip

Two simple rules that will make your home look more respectable. No shoes in the house. No slippers down the pub.

THE KITCHEN

The kitchen is the beating heart of a Mammy's house. Here's where it all happens: meals, big family chats, even the odd conception (there were very few places Redser and I could get any feckin' privacy once we'd filled the place with babbies). And it's where you perform so many of your Mammy chores and duties. Washing. Cleaning. Cooking. And the odd conception.

It's important to keep the kitchen spotless. That way, you can guarantee a healthy family, an orderly house and an immaculate conception.

THE FLOOR

A Mammy's not a Mammy without a bucket and a mop. And her kitchen isn't done until the lino's cleaner than a dentist's Jaguar. You should be able to lick that feckin' floor with your tongue and not only not pick up any germs, but actually get better. That's what all the disinfectant's for. It's basically floor medicine. I've had all my lot down on their hands and knees, lapping at the lino, at the first sign of a bug, and the one thing they always told me down the hospital is that those kids' tongues were feckin' spotless.

One way of telling if your floor's good and clean is if the water in your bucket is feckin' filthy. If it's not, keep going until that water looks like sump oil. You should be able to stand your mop up in it.

And make sure it's a proper feckin' mop. One that looks like a 95-year-old hippie doing a headstand. Not one of these newfangled Super-mops or Spider-mops or Bat-mops or whatever they are. A mop is a mop is a feckin' mop. If it doesn't look like you've stuck the head of the professor fella from *Back to the Future* on a spike, it's not a feckin' mop.

THE OVEN

I saw a van on Wexford Street a few weeks ago and you will not believe what it said on the side: 'M. Stapleton, Oven Cleaner.' Oven cleaner? Oven feckin' cleaner? As a job? And wasn't it a feckin' fellow driving the van?

Two things I want to make ABSOLUTELY FECKIN' CRYSTAL BUCKING CLEAR.

One: oven cleaning is not man's work. You might as well ask a man to have a baby or make a cup of bucking tea.
Two: no one with a feckin' shred of dignity would ever call someone in to clean their oven. That'd be like calling someone in to brush your teeth or wipe your arse. Who

do you think you are? One of those in-bred royal feckers who couldn't even clap without instructions? Have some feckin' self-respect.

And don't buy any of that shite about magical cleaning products. What an oven needs is a good feckin' scrub, every feckin' time you use it. Think about it. What else is there in your home that's regularly stuffed with food and gets used every day? Exactly. Your arse and your mouth. And you wouldn't leave it three months before cleaning either of those, M. Fucking Stapleton.

Our Mark uses the oven to dry his work boots, the cheeky bugger. But they come out cleaner than they went in.

THE KETTLE

If it weren't for Winnie next door, my best friend would be my kettle. I get to missing it if I haven't seen it for a while. I'm going to have my ashes put in mine when I finally can-can off this mortal whatnot. I even took my kettle on jury service with me, just in case. Talk about *Twelve Angry Men*, I tell you, it got pretty steamy in that jury room. It was only the regular tea that kept us going (there was quite a queue for the toilet). But by the time I was through, an innocent man was free. And who was there

to offer that caged bird a cup of tea as he first tasted sweet freedom? Yours truly. And that was when he confessed it was actually him who'd hotwired that milkfloat. And did he thank me? Did he bollocks. Well, that's Buster Brady for you.

Your main problem with your kettle is the limescale. Feckin' horrible stuff. If you don't give your kettle a good servicing regularly, it'll start to look like something you tell the kids to peer into at the seaside, full of exotic rock formations with all weird creatures clinging to the side.

Boiling vinegar does the trick. But mind, because it boils over and makes a right mess. And for feck's sake don't forget you've filled the thing with vinegar. Poor Father Quinn has never forgiven me for that cup of Earl Grey boiling vinegar I made him. Mind you, even he'd admit, his teeth had never been cleaner. He had a smile like Pamela feckin' Anderson when he left, and a voice to match.

THE FREEZER

Defrosting a freezer is a feckin' pain in the arse like no other. It's like waiting for a feckin' comet to come round again. So make sure you've got something else to do all day.

I like to unplug the freezer in the morning and go down the pub. And when I get back at night, I call the fire brigade and get them to pump the water out of the kitchen. (Some of those firemen could pump me out any time. Cathy told me to write that.) Plus, I've half the cleaning of the floor done then, which is what I call killing two birds with one bush.

THE FRIDGE

You should know the fridge door is open by sight, not smell. Open the door. If a little light comes on, that's good. If there's a reek like trench foot, you need to give your fridge a bit more love. Everyone's fridge hums, but it should be the motor, not the salad bin.

Check every day and throw out anything that's past its sell-by date, except smoked meat, which I don't think ever goes off (if old bacon is actually fizzing, throw more lard in the pan to drown out the noise), and cheese – when it goes blue, you can just pretend it's foreign.

But it's the outside of the fridge that counts. Plaster it in so much crap it looks like one of the kiddies brought home a papier maché art project. Postcards from Connemara (Jaysus, even people who live there go there on holiday), pictures of God-knows-what-oh-it's-lovely-darling from the grandkiddies, prescriptions (for conditions you don't mind the neighbours knowing about), lucky Lotto tickets that were only four

THINGS TO DO WITH PEGS

NO.9 | GARDEN PEG GAME

Great for getting kids out in the fresh air. The aim of the game is to put all the pegs on the washing line, and while you're out there, this basket of wet things might as well go up there too. Ahhh. Tea.

numbers short and recipes you've cut out and will never be arsed to make. It's not so much a fridge as a magnetic vertical bin.

And never, ever turn down a fridge magnet. I've got so many magnets on my fridge, if I hold my handbag too close, it wipes my points card. I even got a fridgie from the feckin' undertaker when I buried Redser. A little urn-shaped one. I'm surprised it's not filled with souvenir iron filings so you can make his ashes do a magnetic dance. Express yourself with your fridge display. (If it's impossible to open the door against the pull of the magnets, you've gone too far.)

Mammy's Tip
When chopping onions, stop yourself from crying by drawing funny faces on them.

THE BIN

The best bin is a feckin' big pedal monster. Something about the size of a postbox is right. But not that colour, in case you wake up with a cider head and throw all your letters away.

Never overfill a bin. If you can't reach the top, it's time to change the bag. Unless you've a set of steps, in which case you can probably get another couple of days out of it.

And for feck's sake REMEMBER TO EMPTY IT BEFORE YOU GO AWAY. Jaysus, the stink when we came back after six days at Butlins. Smelled like someone had been boiling John McCririck's vests in the house. Some of the feckin' wallpaper had started to peel. Took us a fortnight with all the windows open before we stopped walking round with rolled-up bits of tissue stuffed up our noses. Turns out a week of unseasonably hot weather can really bring the horror out of a seemingly harmless bundle of chicken giblets, fish skins and sprout peelings.

THE KITCHEN TABLE

Your kitchen table is the command deck of the family, so it needs respect and protection. I use mats. I like to live dangerously. But I've seen plenty who give it the full cocoon. One rubberized fellow, to keep the heat from transferring to the Formica; one easy-wipe fellow, for when there's grandkids doing painting or Plasticine or just chucking their food about like it's feckin' target practice; and one decent bit of cloth to go over the other two to make it look like you've got some standards.

I'd say, keep a picture of what your table looks like under all that armour in case it gets stolen and you need to describe it to the police. Actually, it might already have been pinched, so check. Those tablecloths soak up a lot of shite. They can probably stand up on their own.

BITS AND PIECES

A good **Thermos flask** will eventually taste of chicken soup whatever you put in it. So put chicken soup in it. Even if you want tea. It's all the same in the end.

Chip pans need to be caked in fat like a cross-Channel swimmer. Never try getting that stuff off. It's where all the goodness is. That's the taste of home, that is. You know what I always say? Home is where the heart attack is. Ideally, your chip pan should be the Cliff Richard of your kitchen: about 100 years old and with no original features.

Your **microwave oven** is the work of the devil. Anything that cooks the inside of something before the outside is in league with dark forces. Use sparingly and mainly as an easy place to hide any brown envelopes you can't bring yourself to face. (See my bit on eating and home finances.)

A **toaster** is God's way of letting you gamble without losing money. Your kitchen's very own one-armed bandit. You set the dial to whatever number you like – doesn't matter, because it's like rolling a pair of feckin' dice – and pull down the handle. After that, depending on your luck, you get warm bread, perfect toast or charcoal tiles. The only thing you can guarantee is a ready supply of breadcrumbs. Just upend the feckin' thing and they come pissing out. That's your winnings. Sorry it's in loose change.

Kitchen roll will absorb anything. Anything. If a boatload of it went down in the Irish Sea, you'd be able to walk from Dún Laoghaire to Holyhead without getting your feet wet. Like anyone would want to feckin' visit Holyhead. It'd be like visiting the Museum of God Help Us. You could double the amount of nightlife in Holyhead by going in there after dark with a pot of yoghurt.

The top of your cupboards is a great halfway house between the kitchen and the dump. Anything too big for the bin goes up there.

Remember to dust the shite on top of your cupboards any time you're expecting a visit from a nine-foot-tall relative with a dust allergy who might cut you out of their will, otherwise who the hissing feck gives a pig's bollock? It's the tiny kitchen loft, and it's out of shite, out of mind.

ON TOP OF MY CUPBOARDS:

A plug-in steamer (feck that, what's the use when I've got saucepans and colanders?)

A battery-powered peppermill (there's nothing wrong with my wrists – and if one of them does pack up, Dermot's are like a second pair of fists, the filthy fecker)

A foot spa (if I want bubbles round my feet I'll eat a jar of pickled onions before I get in the bath)

A breadmaker (already got one of those – called Hovis)

A salmon kettle (nobody's ever asked me for a two-foot-wide cup of tea)

A smoothie maker (I don't even know what this is – in my day a smoothie was a fellow with brilliantine in his hair who wouldn't take a slap in the chops for an answer – and it's a bit late for me to be making one of those)

A Veg-O-Matic, a Chop-O-Matic and about four other Feck-O-Matics

A pasta maker (some daft feckin' present from Hilary that looks like a cross between a mangle and a photocopier – it's all very well making your own pasta, but how do you get it in the feckin' tins?)

A soda siphon (or it might be an unbranded fire extinguisher – not sure)

A salad spinner (if you're living off salad, you won't have enough energy to wind the feckin' thing up to get it going)

MAMMY'S CALENDAR

Every Mammy needs a calendar, for all those important dates – birthdays, hair appointments, anniversaries, hair appointments, bank holidays, hair appointments, haircuts, that sort of thing. (I have to plan my hair appointments in advance. Not the booking, the conversation. That Rita's a lovely girl and she does a decent blow-dry, but she's like a feckin' stuck record. Says the same three things all the time. She might be a robot. Anyway, I don't let her get a word in edgeways now. A Mammy is always prepared.)

Don't bother with any of the free calendars from the local takeaways – there's no room for writing because of the feckin' great picture of a Chinese mountain or a monkey in the mist. Sure you don't want a sweaty ape staring down at you from your wall when you've Grandad in the room next door.

I get my calendars from Father Quinn, in return for a donation to the church cover-up fund.

THINGS TO DO WITH PEGS

NO.10 | ADVENT CALENDAR

Open your peg and what's inside! A chocolate, just like in the Bible.

January

*'A smile can warm
even the coldest day'*

Mon	Tues	Wed	Thur	Fri	Sat	Sun
31	1 New Year's Day St Basil's Day	2 St Odilo's Day *10am HAIR - talk about Xmas*	3 St Genevieve's Day	4 St Roger's Day	5 St Convoyon's Day	6 St Erminold's Day
7 St Tillo's Day	8 St Frodobert's Day	9 St Julian's Day	10 St William's Day	11 St Brettiva's Day	12 St Benedict's Day	13 St Kentigern's Day
14 St Pontianus's Day	15 St Tarsitia's Day	16 St Dacian's Day *10am HAIR - talk about weather*	17 St Genulf's Day	18 St Leobard's Day	19 St Branvalator's Day	20 St Henry's Day
21 St Meginrad's Day	22 St Ulphus's Day	23 St Maimbod's Day	24 St Eric's Day	25 St Poppo's Day	26 St Polycarp's Day *Rory's B/Day*	27 St Paula's Day
28 St Cyril's Day	29 St Voloc's Day	30 St Glascian's Day *10am HAIR - talk about what a long month it's been*	31 St Torquatus's Day	1	2	3

February

'Happiness is like jam: best thickly spread'

Mon	Tues	Wed	Thur	Fri	Sat	Sun
28	29	30	31	1 St Bridget's Day	2 St Lawrence's Day	3 St Wendelin's Day *Post St Vodoald's Day cards?*
4 St Lifard's Day	5 St Vodoald's Day	6 St Brinolph's Day	7 St Tresain's Day	8 St Cuthman's Day	9 St Attracta's Day	10 St Erlulph's Day
11 St Fritheswida's Day	12 St Eulalia's Day Shrove Tuesday *Eat As Much Chocolate As Poss Before Lent*	13 St Fusca's Day Ash Wednesday Lent begins *11 am HAIR – talk about ANYTHING EXCEPT chocolate*	14 St Auxentius's Day	15 St Ebbo's Day	16 St Onesimus's Day	17 St Henry's Day
18 St Colmann's Day	19 St Gall's Day *WEEK WITHOUT CHOCOLATE – THAT'S ENOUGH*	20 St Mildred's Day	21 St Pepin's Day	22 St Baradat's Day	23 St Milburga's Day	24 St Praetextatus's Day
25 St Guinefortus's Day	26 St Agricola's Day	27 St Baldomer's Day *10 am HAIR – pretend you're still off the chocolate*	28 St Oswald's Day	1	2	3

What's that you say? Cup of tea? Don't mind if I do.

Stain remover also removes telltale stains from Dermot's toothbrush.

How will I get my shopping home in this?

Stage one: the surface clean.

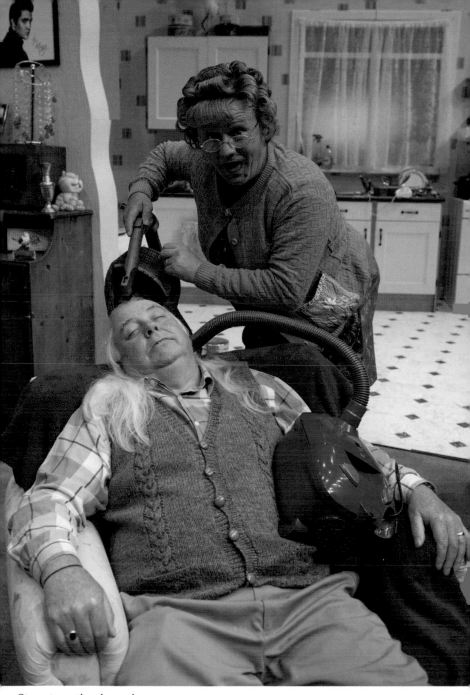

Stage two: the deep clean.
If you don't have time for this, just sweep the dust under the cap.

Family recipe for a hot toddy.

March

 'Love is its own reward'

Mon	Tues	Wed	Thur	Fri	Sat	Sun
25	26	27	28	1 St David's Day	2 St Chad's Day	3 St Cunigundus's Day *So that's what it's named after!*
4 St Focus's Day *You'll be lucky if you can feckin' see after a day of Cunigundus*	5 St Phocas's Day	6 St Fridolin's Day	7 St Paul The Simple's Day	8 St Gay's Day *TELL RORY*	9 St Poncius's Day	10 St Kessog's Day Mothering Sunday *Buy cornflakes* *GET SOMEONE ELSE TO*
11 St Gumpert's Day	12 St Maximilian's Day	13 St Mocheomoc's Day *10 am HAR – talk about the weather or some shite*	14 St Eupergius's Day	15 St Zachary's Day	16 St Heribert's Day	17 St Patrick's Day
18 St Finian's Day St Patrick's Day (observed)	19 St Alcmund's Day	20 St Wulfram's Day	21 St Serapian's Day	22 St Frumence's Day	23 St Turibius's Day	24 St Pygmenius's Day Palm Sunday
25 St Cammin's Day *Buy Easter eggs*	26 St Dismas's Day *Buy more Easter eggs to replace ones Grandad's eaten*	27 St Adalpret's Day *DAVID'S B-DAY* *10 am HAR – talk about Easter*	28 St Guntram's Day Maundy Thursday	29 Good Friday	30 Easter Saturday	31 Easter Sunday Irish Standard Time begins

April

'Men are made
by women'

Oh so men are OUR fault?

FECK OFF WITH YOU

Mon	Tues	Wed	Thur	Fri	Sat	Sun
1 Easter Monday *GRAND NATIONAL*	**2** Easter Tuesday	**3** Easter Wednesday	**4** Easter Thursday	**5** St Beccan's Day	**6** St Celsus McAedh's Day *2.30 p.m. DENTIST*	**7** St Aibert's Day
8 St Albert's Day	**9** St Dotto's Day	**10** St Godobert's Day *10 a.m. HAIR – talk about Easter again*	**11** St Guthlac's Day *BONO'S B-DAY*	**12** St Erkenbodo's Day	**13** St Hermenegild's Day	**14** St Ledwina's Day
15 St Peter Gonzales's Day	**16** St Anicetus's Day	**17** St Simeon's Day	**18** St Laserian's Day	**19** St Ursmar's Day	**20** St Serf's Day	**21** St Victor's Day
22 St Opportuna's Day	**23** St George's Day	**24** St Norbert's Day *10 a.m. HAIR – talk about the bingo*	**25** St Floribert's Day	**26** St Trudpert's Day	**27** St Zita's Day	**28** St Pollio's Day
29 St Hoildis's Day	**30** St Erconwald's Day	1	2	3	4	5

May

*'There is no horizon –
there is only forever'*

Mon	Tues	Wed	Thur	Fri	Sat	Sun
29	30	1 St Brioc's Day	2 St Walbert's Day	③ St Genius's Day *TRY PRIZE CROSSWORD*	4 St Godehard's Day	5 St Gengulf's Day
6 May Day	7 St Mastidia's Day	8 St Odrian's Day *10 am. HAIR – pretend you've lost your voice*	9 St Suitbert's Day	10 St Mamertus's Day	11 St Majolus's Day	12 St Modoald's Day *CATHY'S B-DAY*
13 St John the Silent's Day	14 St Audoenus's Day	15 St Wigbert's Day	16 St Ragnobert's Day	17 St Maw's Day	18 St Potamon's Day	19 St Ivo's Day
20 St Austregisil's Day	21 St Godrick's Day	22 St Rita's Day *10 am. HAIR – pretend you've still got no voice*	23 St Andrew Bobola's Day	24 St Dominic's Day	25 St Dumhade's Day	26 St Oduvald's Day
27 St Seraphion's Day	28 St John Shirt's Day *Sounds like a jumble sale*	29 St Sissinius's Day *I hope the poor fecker didn't have a lisp*	30 St Maguil's Day	31 St Petronilla's Day	1	2

June

'Birdsong is Our Lord whistling while he works' ~~He gets up too feckin' early~~

Mon	Tues	Wed	Thur	Fri	Sat	Sun
27	28	29	30	31	**1** St Justin's Day *Buy gloves, mask, worming tablets + spout. Van for tomorrow*	**2** St Peter's Day *GRANDAD'S ANNUAL BATH (WARN NEIGHBOURS)*
3 St Kevin's Day Bank Holiday *CLEAN BATHROOM* ←	**4** St Ninnoc's Day	**5** St Illidius's Day *10 a.m. HAIR – talk about Grandad's bath*	**6** St Jarlath's Day	**7** St Godeschalc's Day	**8** St Chlodulph's Day *LEAVE BATHROOM TO AIR*	**9** St Alexander's Day *CLEAN BATHROOM AGAIN JUST TO BE SURE* →
10 St Jodocus's Day *THE TRIPLETS B-DAY – 1 card or 3?*	**11** St Tochumra's Day	**12** St Odulph's Day	**13** St Felicola's Day	**14** St Dogmael's Day	**15** St Vitus's Day	**16** St Benno's Day Father's Day
17 St Arsacius Day *Grandad's patron saint?*	**18** St Amand's Day	**19** St Sebastian Newdigate's Day *10 a.m. HAIR – pretend you've still got no voice*	**20** St Bain's Day	**21** St Ralph's Day	**22** St Aaron's Day	**23** St Ediltrudis's Day
24 St Bartholomew's Day	**25** St Radbod's Day	**26** St Raingarda's Day	**27** St Hilary's Day *She's no fucking saint*	**28** St Marcella's Day	**29** St Emma's Day	**30** St Martial's Day

July

'A tender word can open a ~~locked heart~~ PINT PAIR OF LEGS*'*

Mon	Tues	Wed	Thur	Fri	Sat	Sun
1 St Cybar's Day *SEND TREVOR'S B-DAY CARD*	**2** St Otto's Day	**3** St Appolin's Day *10 a.m. HAIR – pretend you've been on holiday (Corradoe?)*	**4** St Bolcan's Day	**5** St Modwina's Day	**6** St Sexburgis's Day *BETTY'S B-DAY*	**7** St Degga's Day
8 St Adrian Fortescue's Day	**9** St Agilulf's Day	**10** St Etto's Day	**11** St Hyldulf's Day	**12** St Prejectus's Day *TREVOR'S B/DAY*	**13** St Thurial's Day	**14** St Vigor's Day
15 St Swithuns' Day	**16** St Osmund's Day	**17** St Turninus's Day *10 a.m. HAIR – talk about Trevor*	**18** St Bruno's Day	**19** St Martin's Day	**20** St Thorlac's Day	**21** St Zoticus's Day
22 St Wandregisil's Day	**23** St Birgitta's Day	**24** St Kinga's Day	**25** St Nissen's Day	**26** St Pastor's Day	**27** St Paul's Day	**28** St Botwid's Day *Half these feckin' names are made up*
29 St Ladislas's Day	**30** St Julitta's Day	**31** St Neotus's Day *10 a.m. HAIR – talk about how hot it is*	1	2	3	4

August

'A prayer is more than a wish; it is a superwish'

Mon	Tues	Wed	Thur	Fri	Sat	Sun
29	30	31	1 St Sativola's Day	2 St Alban's Day	3 St Gamaliel's Day	4 St Sigrada's Day
5 St Fredulph's Day Bank Holiday	6 St Sixtus's Day	7 St Cajetan's Day	8 St Osonans's Day	9 St Fedlimin's Day	10 St Blane's Day	11 St Rusticola's Day
12 St Muredach's Day	13 St Radegundis's Day	14 St Werenfrid's Day *10 a.m. HAIR* *Rita on holiday – RELAX*	15 St MacCartin's Day	16 St Roch's Day *MARK'S B-DAY*	17 St Hiero's Day	18 St Helena's Day
19 St Cumin's Day	20 St Bernard's Day *↑ Every dog has its day!*	21 St Reginwald's Day	22 St Symphoranius's Day	23 St Ebba's Day	24 St Irchard's Day	25 St Adalbert's Day
26 St Zephyrin's Day	27 St Felix's Day	28 St Hermes's Day *10 a.m. HAIR* *– ask Rita about holiday* *(no need to listen) Blow dry?*	29 St Sebbi's Day	30 St Heribert's Day	31 St Ebregisil's Day	1

September

'Every yesterday started out as a bright young tomorrow'

Mon	Tues	Wed	Thur	Fri	Sat	Sun
26	27	28	29	30	31	1 St Fiacre's Day
30 St Leupard's Day						
2 St Prisco's Day	3 St Remaco's Day	4 St Frodoald's Day	5 St Bertin's Day	6 St Pambo's Day	7 St Gunzelinus's Day *MARIA'S B-DAY*	8 St Disibodus's Day
9 St Moswenna's Day *Start mentioning birthday*	10 St Othger's Day *Keep mentioning birthday*	11 *Feckin' U2 set everywhere* St Bodo's Day *10 am HAIR – talk about the days getting shorter* *Say you had hair done for upcoming birthday*	12 St Eanswide's Day *Say you don't want any fuss for birthday*	13 St Anthony's Day *Remind kids Dunne's is open late for BUYING ANY LAST MINUTE STUFF*	14 St Cormac's Day *Call it BIRTHDAY WEEKEND a lot*	15 ★ Aichard's **MAMMY'S BIRTHDAY!**
16 St Eufemia's Day *Take Hilary's present back for refund*	17 St Liofard's Day	18 St Speosippus's Day St Eleiosippus's Day St Meleosippus's Day *↑ Triplet saints!*	19 St Lambert's Day *WMME'S B-DAY – Usual whiskey*	20 St Matthew's Day	21 St Maura's Day	22 St Maurice's Day
23 St Thecla's Day	24 St Geremar's Day	25 St Fimbert's Day *10 am HAIR – talk about B-Day MAKE IT UP* *Remind kids it's Grandad's B-Day tomorrow*	26 St Fimbert's Day *GRANDAD'S 140th B-DAY* *Remind Grandad it's his B-Day today*	27 St Fimbert's Day	28 St Doda's Day	29 St Lutwin's Day

71

October

'May all your autumns be golden'
GET THE WORDS RIGHT
BING FECKIN' CROSBY

Mon	Tues	Wed	Thur	Fri	Sat	Sun
30	1 St Wasnulf's Day	2 St Thomas's Day	3 St Ludger's Day	4 St Ammon's Day	5 St Charitine's Day	6 St Mark's Day
7 St Wolfgang's Day	8 St Reparata's Day	9 St Arnoald's Day *10 a.m. HAIR – talk about Christmas shopping (RITA DOES HERS EARLY)*	10 St Tancha's Day	11 St Tenenan's Day	12 St Cletus's Day	13 St Simpert's Day
14 St Andragisma's Day	15 St Cognoganus's Day	16 St Walderic's Day *Spartacus's B-DAY*	17 St Ambrose's Day	18 St Mono's Day	19 St Ethbin's Day	20 St Sindulf's Day
21 St Viator's Day	22 St Philip's Day	23 St Theoderic's Day *10 a.m. HAIR talk about clocks going back*	24 St Maglorius's Day	25 St Lupus's Day	26 St Afra's Day	27 St Abban's Day Irish Standard Time ends
28 St Faro's Day Bank Holiday	29 St Narcissus's Day	30 St Serapion's Day	31 St Bega's Day	1	2	3

November

 *'A hearth is a heart in all but name'*

Mon	Tues	Wed	Thur	Fri	Sat	Sun
28	29	30	31	1 All Saints' Day ↑ *That's a LOT of feckin' saints*	2 St Vulgan's Day	3 St Hubert's Day
4 St Birstan's Day	5 St Winnoc's Day	6 St Illtyd's Day *10 a.m. HAR - talk about Strictly*	7 St Willibrord's Day	8 St Godfrey's Day	9 St John's Day	10 St Ludmilla's Day Remembrance Day
11 St Menas's Day	12 St Thorkill's Day	13 St Constant's Day	14 St Clementine's Day	15 St Richard Whiting's Day *THEY MADE THE FELLA OFF COUNTDOWN A SAINT?*	16 St Othmar's Day	17 St Anianus's Day *Patron saint of PILES?*
18 St Hilda's Day	19 St Quintian's Day	20 St Silvester's Day *10 a.m. HAR talk about X Factor*	21 St Rufus's Day	22 St Theodore the Studite's Day	23 St Felicity's Day	24 St Kenan's Day
25 St Erasmus's Day	26 St Nicon's Day	27 St Cungar's Day	28 St Silas's Day	29 St Cuthbert Mayne's Day	30 St Andrew's Day	1

December

'Treat every kiss as if it were your first'

YEAH SMACK HIM IN THE FACE WITH YOUR HANDBAG

Mon	Tues	Wed	Thur	Fri	Sat	Sun
25	26	27	28	29	30	1 St Nessan's Day
30 St Perpetuus's Day	31 *DIET STARTS* New Year's Eve St Marius's Day					
2 St Bibiana's Day	3 St Firminus's Day	4 St Barbara's Day *10 a.m. HAIR –* *say you've done* *Christmas shopping*	5 St Birinus's Day *Do Christmas shopping*	6 St Nicholas's Day *Do more Christmas* *shopping*	7 St Babolen's Day *Order TURKEY* *from* *Bloody O'Riordan*	8 St Romaric's Day *Get Mark to get* *DECORATIONS out* *of loft*
9 St Gerontius's Day *Get Dermot to* *'FIND' a tree*	10 St Gausbert's Day *PUT TREE +* *DECS UP*	11 St Daniel's Day	12 St Valeric's Day	13 St Lucy's Day	14 St Spiridion's Day	15 St Odilda's Day
16 St Beanus's Day	17 St Lazarus's Day *Turn Mattress*	18 St Wunibald's Day *10 a.m. HAIR –* *talk about* *Christmas*	19 St Nemesion's Day *Buy Christmas Cake* *(SAY YOU MADE IT)*	20 St Unsicinus's Day *Buy ALL THE* *SPROUTS IN* *QUINNS*	21 St Edburghe's Day *PICK UP* *TURKEY*	22 *WRAP PRESENTS* St Gregory's Day *Cut Sellotape into hundreds* *of 6" strips* *Lightly stick strips* *all over Grandad*
23 St Mazota's Day	24 Christmas Eve	25 Christmas Day *EAT YOUR Feckin'* *SELF SILLY*	26 St Stephen's Day *Start leftovers*	27 St Zoilus's Day *Make Leftovers Soup* *Freeze first two gallons*	28 St Theodore's Day *Make Leftovers* *Surprise*	29 St Ebrulf's Day *Finish leftovers* *Give rest of* *cake to Grandad* *Stand back*

DR. AGNES BROWN
presents

Mammy's Guide to Having Kids

A wiser head than me once said, 'Give me the child who says the funniest things and I'll show you how to go placidly amongst the noise and haste.' Or something like that. Winnie's got it on a plate in her toilet.

Many's the Mammy who's been pushed to the limit by her little ones and considered selling them for experiments. The main thing is to keep your head, even if all about you are off theirs.

Remember: children are a gift. Except you can't get your money back on the feckers if they don't suit you.

Behaviour

1 *Tantrums*

Meltdowns, wobblies, shit fits, call them what you like. Some people call them paddies, but that's not the sort of language you'll hear round our street unless you want to see some proper feckin' tantrums.

Whoever does your Photoshop
YOU'RE FIRED.

You've got to show a child that you're the boss.
Try pointing at them when they won't do as they're told and shouting, 'You're fired!'

MAMMY'S TIP

Put a bucket over baby's head. They'll soon quiet down.

❷ *Giving Up the Dummy*

Once a kid's got hooked on a dummy, it's hard to get the thing out. I remember Cathy loved the taste of rubber in her mouth. I was worried she'd keep the habit into adulthood, but Winnie says it's safer that way, whatever the feck that means.

How to break the habit?
If you're sterilizing the dummy in one of them steam machines, double up and do your sprouts in it. Anything coming out of that thing won't be staying in the little one's mouth for long.

Maggie Grainger used to dip her Brian's dummy in gin. He's 46 and he stills prefers it straight from the optic. He can't sleep without a bellyful of the stuff, but I tell you, he's not had the colic since '74.

3 Thumb-sucking

As long as they've grown out of it by the time they're old enough to smoke, you're all right. Otherwise, they can do awful damage trying to light their thumbs after a few bevvies.

4 Cleaning Their Teeth

If you don't want the little ones to spend half their life upside down in a dentist's chair while he goes drilling for tin, you've got to get them brushing their teeth. Mind you, if you don't, you'll save them a fortune in toothpowder when they get a nice false set.

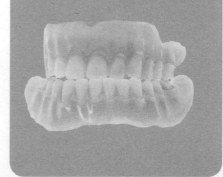

5 Getting Their Bits Out in Front of People

Kids are the most terrible show-offs. Flashing their shop-fronts to all and sundry. I used to worry my Trevor would grow up to be some sort of bus stop pervert, waggling his banger and beans at the queue without a by-your-leave.

They all seem to grow out of it. I don't like to boast about my parenting skills, but I can say with my hand on my heart, that, to the best of my knowledge, none of mine have become flashers.

What happened to flashers? It used to be all the rage. Sure, you couldn't move for them when I was a girl.

My Mammy used to drag me down the shops wearing a set of feckin' blinkers.

There was Mackerel Mick, Tommy the Tent, Parkie Padraig, the conductor of the 92 bus *(upstairs only)*, Bushes Duffy, Tripod O'Leary, Boner Mahoney, Signpost Flynn, Spudsack O'Farrell.

Ah, you don't get characters like that any more. I blame them blue channels on the satellite box I've heard exist nowadays, with all your greased-up lads flapping their truncheon meat at you for money. They've ruined the mystery. Redser always hated it when an amateur sport went professional.

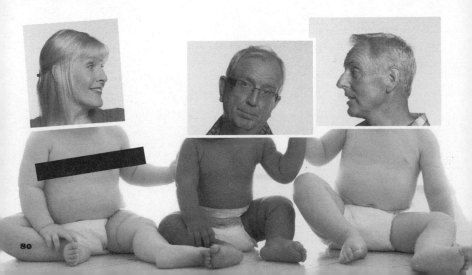

⑥ The Naughty Step

I never held with the whole 'naughty step' thing. It takes five minutes to put them on the naughty step, and only a second to clout them round the naughty ear with a naughty tea towel.

And what if you've a bungalow? It's a feckin' step too far is what it is.

Plus, leave them on the stairs and you have to keep stepping over them. I tried putting Dermot on the naughty step once for leaving a roller skate on the stairs. Forgot he was there and, sure enough, two hours later didn't I nearly break my feckin' neck?

Out of sight, out of mind, I say. There's always the naughty loft or the naughty cupboard.

Mind you don't put them on the naughty shelf – you know, the one where you keep *The Joy Of S-E-K-S* and the Jilly Coopers. You don't want them getting ideas.

Whatever you do, and wherever you live, don't put them in the naughty cellar. It's got all sorts of connotations since that Spritzer Fritzer fella.

⑦ Fussy Eating

Toddlers are always making a fuss about something on their plates – usually tomatoes. They might have a point, you know. I've changed enough nappies to know that most of a tomato goes straight through without touching the sides. You've as much chance of digesting a feckin' screwdriver as a tomato pip.

Mind you, Winnie says she can think of worse things to put in her mouth, and they haven't even got pips. Unless there's something going round.

Anyway, if it's a fussy eater you've got, or a conscientious objector, or just a wilful little shite, hide the food.

FOODSTUFF	HOW TO HIDE (per serving)	Rating (%)
Fish	Easy: straight into the mash. Remember to remove the heads first, though. An eye staring up at you from the top of your little potato-mountain is enough to put anyone off dinner for life.	95
Sprouts	Dip them in chocolate and say they're Welsh toffees.	20
Tomatoes	Cover them in ketchup and say it's just a bit lumpy.	60
Greens	Add them to anything brown: gravy, Marmite, chocolate sponge.	40
Liver	Don't even feckin' bother. A kid would know liver at 250 metres even if it'd been vapourized and a light mist of it sprayed near the jar that the jam inside a doughnut came in.	0.001
Cheese	Sticks to the underside of anything: bacon, waffles, rice cakes. It'd probably stick to the underneath of soup if you could find it.	84
Cabbage	Depends how small you chop it up. If you can shred it really fine, you can hide it in lime jelly. My record is getting some into a Smartie.	29
Eggs	Scramble them, add blue colouring, and tell them it's Superman's superfood. Don't add brown colouring: you've never seen anything so much like a pavement pattie in your life. People three streets away were retching.	12
Brandy	Put it in a bottle marked 'creosote' and hide it under the sink. Kids don't touch what they can't spell.	99

Sleep

God love them, kids, but they're not born to sleep, are they? It's as if they're making up for those nine quiet months in the dark by having nine deafening months with the light on.

① Swaddling

If you didn't see that one coming, you need a feckin eye test

When they're newborns, it's all about the swaddling. You have to wrap the little buggers up like Tutankhamun. Talk about the Mammy's curse.

Swaddling takes a bit of learning. It's like bucking origami. But you'll get the hang of it after the first couple of hours of screaming. If you're lucky, you might not even scream that long.

Redser tried using parcel tape when he couldn't get the blanket round Mark. He was drunk, bless him. I could tell because he'd stuck two stamps on the poor babby's forehead.

Sometimes it's tempting to swaddle them round the head, just to try to muffle the feckin' noise. By the time you've finished, it's like a game of pass the parcel and the prize in the middle is a police siren.

Rocking them is another way. It's hell on your arms if they're a big old unit, though. And I don't know how Dermot and Maria manage with the triplets. They've only the four arms. Still, you learn unexpected skills as a parent, and the circus will always need jugglers.

Put this in a more relevant section, it's not just a page filler

THINGS TO DO WITH PEGS

NO.1 | SEALING A BAG OF SALAD

Keeps salad safely in the crisper until it rots and can be thrown away.

Green Salad

❷ Controlled Crying

This is what all the young mothers talk about now. Controlled crying. Controlled crying. Controlled feckin' crying. I wish they'd control their feckin' bleating about it.

Don't ask me what it is. Babby cries because it can't feckin' talk. A bit like Grandad when his pills kick in. Maybe they fit the little ones with volume controls on the maternity ward.

I used to find singing them a little song was enough to stop them crying. Something traditional, handed down the generations, like . . .

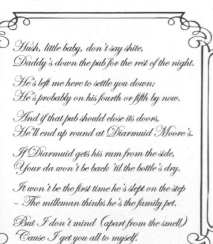

Hush, little baby, don't say shite,
Daddy's down the pub for the rest of the night.

He's left me here to settle you down;
He's probably on his fourth or fifth by now.

And if that pub should close its doors,
He'll end up round at Diarmuid Moore's.

If Diarmuid gets his rum from the side,
Your da won't be back 'til the bottle's dry.

It won't be the first time he's slept on the step
– The milkman thinks he's the family pet.

But I don't mind (apart from the smell)
Cause I get you all to myself.

It's even better with the accordion.

❸ Night Terrors

Night terrors? Jaysus, I've had my share of those. Grandad getting the wrong door and leaving me with a laundry basket full of nightwater. Redser screaming himself awake because he dreamt he was being fed to a giant Terry Wogan.

The kiddies get the terrible heebeegeebees as well. Young Cathy used to wake up in a shocking state: sweating, shivering, unable to speak. Dermot still does, the morning after a lock-in at Foley's.

I used to bring them into my bed sometimes, but Redser's arse would disturb them. God knows, he loved colcannon, but it fucking punished him. It was an abusive relationship. Like that Mike and Tina Turner. Redser's gas was so powerful, I once saw him fart a Venus flytrap shut. Some nights I'd wake up, freezing to my bones, and find the bedclothes on the other side of the room, smoking slightly.

If they get it at the weekend, it's Saturday Night Fever

Potty Training

When they're little ones, you change their nappies and they pee all over you with big grins on their silly faces. 'Getting you back for the baptism,' Redser used to say. From the other side of the room, in his oilskins.

All mine were done with terry nappies and a big old pin. It was a lot more washing, sure, but you learn pretty quickly that blood comes out at about sixty.

Pull-ups aren't bad for babbies. And if you rinse them out and put them on the line, they're good for another few goes. Once is not enough at that price. And if it's good enough for Grandad, it's good enough for the chisellers.

Try rewarding the little ones for getting to the loo on time with a Smartie or something. Sure, you'd think not walking round in a nappy full of backdoor pudding was enough of a reward on its own . . .

Of course, you can always give them a bit of time with their bits swinging in the breeze – keeps the sores off – but if you do, put them in the garden where you're less likely to go arse over tit when you slip in a puddle of piss.

And with kids, remember the golden rule:

Little accidents will happen. Three of my lot were little accidents.

Dry nights: the bullseye. There's those throwaway sheets you can get for the bed. But a towel or half a kitchen roll is just as good. Or any baking disasters – an overdone flan base stretched out with a rolling pin, or out-of-date cheesecake base mix. They're both surprisingly absorbent.

My Redser was going to make a whole kiddy's mattress out of that green foamy stuff you stick artificial flowers in. Never got round to it.

He had a lot of plans before he passed. Like the colander that lets the lumps out but leaves the liquid in. And the remote-controlled

remote control, so he didn't have to get out of his chair to get the remote control. All he managed in the end were a couple of shelves and half a go-kart (left-hand side).

He said he wanted to leave his mark. And he did, if you count all the feckin' pencil marks he put up the wall before doing those shelves.

But, you know, he may not have given the world the internet or the stay-pressed shirt, but through our beautiful children, and the grandchildren they've given me, Redser did leave his Mark in this world after all. And his Cathy. And his Trevor. And his Dermot. And his Rory. And his Conor.

Or was that one of Bernadette MacLean's?

Coughs
& Sneezes

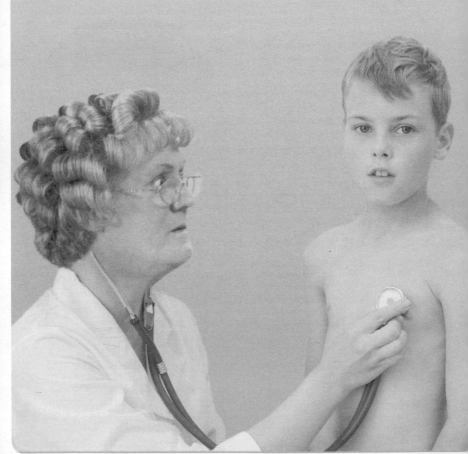

① Chicken Pox

Chicken pox is a feckin' curse. Bless him, when our Mark had it, he looked like the side of a boat. Barnacles all over the poor mite. I put so much calamine lotion on the poor sod, Winnie thought I'd been plastering over the holes in him. Ginny Fogarty looked the same when she got married. But that's because she'd had a shiteload of miniatures at her hen do and fallen asleep on a sunbed wearing that moth-eaten onesie.

You can keep the little ones from scratching by telling them the spots are buttons that they mustn't press or their ears'll fall off. If they don't buy that – and our Dermot didn't – tell them they get a new spot every time they tell a lie. If they don't buy that – and our Dermot didn't – it serves the little feckers right if they end up looking like they've been attacked by gulls. *Our Dermot still doesn't buy much. He tends to come by it for free.*

② Threadworms

The less said about this department the better. Besides, all you do as a new mam is talk about your pride and joy's arsefudge. You come up with nicknames for the more traumatic ones. You know. The Apoocalypse. The Poonami. Mammy's Little Pooicide Bomber.

③ ADHD

I've no bucking idea what this is. Is it an internet thing? I think Cathy said something about an ADHD cable for the TV. I wasn't really listening. I was just as bad at school. I'm sure there must be a word for it.

④ Headlice

Rotten little feckers, headlice. I swear they put them in the drinking fountains at school. No one ever had headlice till they went to school. Teachers must be riddled with the things. It's no wonder they only wear second-hand clothes.

You can buy that wicked anti-nit muck at the chemist's that smells like a cross between Dettol and moonshine, and I did a couple of times, but Grandad caught wind of it and that was that.

They say headlice are a sign of clean hair. But that's a feckin' weird definition of clean, if there's lice crawling all over it. It's one rule for hair, another for cocks, by the feckin' sound of it.

⑤ Car Sickness

Our Dermot used to get terrible car sickness as a kiddie. Especially when he was reversing. And it didn't matter whose wheels he'd borrowed, he'd always throw up in the police car on the way home.

Keep a tin of boiled sweets in the car. Apparently you can suppress the gag reflex if you put something hard in your mouth and suck, if you believe the graffiti in the Ladies in Foley's.

⑥ Speech Development

Mark's first word was 'Mammy'. So was Rory's. Dermot's was 'Fuck'. But you can't blame him. I had three sons by then. They just copy what they hear.

Sibling Rivalry

① Sharing a Bedroom

Ours was never a mansion, but we made the best of what we had. Mark and Rory shared a bed when they were toddlers. Then Trevor came along and he had a cot in the same room. When Cathy came along, Redser turned the cot into a bunk cot, with one babby on each level. Then Dermot came along, which was a problem. Redser offered to make five narrow beds, but he drew it on a beer mat and it looked like the back room at Mooney's funeral parlour.

But by then some of the kids were sleeping around. At friends' houses, I mean. One way or another, we managed. You'd be surprised how easy it is to persuade a child that you've made them their own den just by writing DEN in chalk on the gas meter cupboard under the stairs.

② Sharing

Kids are competitive. You've seen piglets round a sow? It was like that round our place of a breakfast, but noisier. It even smelled of feckin' bacon.

'The devil rides in on a horse called Jealousy.' I've got that embroidered on a cushion. So you have to be fair. If you buy one of them an ice-cream, they can feckin' well share with the others. What do you think I am? Made of money?

And as for dividing a cake, that's easy. One slice each.

Grandad gets to lick the plate.
Spartacus gets to lick Grandad

MARK	CATHY'S MAMMY
MARK'S MAMMY	CATHY
RORY	DERMOT'S MAMMY
RORY'S MAMMY	DERMOT
TREVOR	TREVOR'S MAMMY

School

③ How to Tell a Child You're Pregnant

There's different ways of doing this. 'Mammy's eaten a baby pill, and now there's one growing in her tummy' was what I told Mark when I was carrying Rory. 'Da says you're up the duff,' was what he said, bless his heart.

I remember Mark walked in on me and Redser once when we were… you know… making the beast with two backs. Having a grown-up cuddle. Doing S-E-K-S. He asked what we were doing, and Redser said, quick as a flash, 'Practising for the forward roll competition.' We never did it in the kitchen again after that. Besides, that table had one leg shorter than the others and I was worried we'd end up in the cellar with all the knocking those tiles took.

Eventually the kids get used to you expecting. I was popping them out like a Gatling gun in those days. I didn't see my feckin' feet for the best part of ten years. I've lost count of the number of times I left the house in my feckin' slippers.

School is where they learn those valuable social skills: moneymaking, backbiting and snogging. Between these useful lessons, there's the more specialist stuff: adding up, colouring in, capital cities – that sort of nonsense.

I never got on with this one teacher, Miss Turlough. She was a nasty piece of work, but a specialist; she had three different sizes of Bible to whack you with.

She once asked me what the capital of France was. I pointed to the map and said it was a feckin' great F. She said, *'You'll get nothing in the exam for cheek.'* I said, *'I'll get nothing in the exam for knowing the feckin' capital of France. You're meant to be teaching us metalwork.'* I got the large-print Bible for that. And a feckin' great F of my own.

The two worst things for any kid about going to school are bullying and reports. You don't want some vindictive great thug acting the feckin' big man, making you feel small, frightening you from wanting to go to school at all. And bullying's no better.

I swear bullying's got worse since they started all the texting one another. Our Dermot was never off his mobile. I said to him, 'Your thumbs'll fall off if you carry on like that.' Our Mark said, 'He's lucky. It was going blind in my day.'

It's the modern world, I suppose. Everything changes. But I think about modern bullying what I think about modern S-E-K-S: it was better when they had to do it to your face.

The golden rule is that bullies can't win if you don't react. If you let them know they've got to you, you've lost. That's what I told my Rory when he got picked on for not wanting to get his football boots dirty: look like you don't care. If you can manage it, try to fall asleep while they're kicking you.

And I always told my lot, no matter how much someone provokes you, don't hit back. **Hit first. Then they're not expecting it.**

I know violence doesn't solve anything. But in the absence of a solution, it's a great way to keep fit. And it gets them out in the fresh air.

My school reports were a bucking disgrace, so it was always hard for me to have a go at the kids when they came home, trembling, clutching an envelope with more Fs in it than a feckin' gangster film.

It's not like I'm going to stop loving them because they can't do vulgar fractions. I tell you, there's enough vulgarity about without teaching them it in school.

Look at me. I'm head of one of the most respected families in our street, with a downstairs toilet and both sorts of Cinzano, and the only certificate I've got to my name is the one on the market stall that says there's no ratshit on the satsumas. If I'm proof of anything, I'm proof there's things they can't teach you in school. Love. Responsibility. French.

But I suppose they have to grade the poor kids, if only so you can find out if they've been playing hooky down the arcade, selling the old bootleg DVDVs out of a hold-all. I imagine the school governors want to make sure of that with their own kids as much as any of us do. Though I remember you could find out just as easily by shaking Dermot's trackie bottoms off the floor where he left them every feckin' night. If a load of twenties fell out, he probably didn't pick them up in double feckin' maths.

School reports are a load of gobbledegook if you ask me. But take it from Mammy, if you can translate them, you're fine so. All it takes is a bit of interpretating.

What they say	What they mean
'Tries his best'	Thicko
'Could try harder'	No feckin' idea who this kid is, so I'll hedge me bets
'A+'	The little bollix won't leave me alone
'Unsatisfactory'	Thicko
'Excellent detail'	Tiny feckin' handwriting like a serial killer
'His coursework was exemplary'	His exam results will be shite
'Good attendance'	At least he turned up
'A credit to the school'	One day I'll owe him money
'He'll go far'	Hopefully out of Ireland
'Satisfactory'	We didn't move him up a set
'Charming'	I'm the art teacher and I fancy him
'I only wish he spent as much time on his studies as he did cultivating friends'	He's a nice kid, but he's still a THICKO

Teenagers

Bringing up a child, there is one certainty. That, after all the love, the sleepless nights, the nappies full of shite and the tenderly dried tears, one day your little bundle of joy will turn to you with that special look in their eyes, and tell you, with all their heart, to *fuck off*.

It's one of those special moments. It means they're finally a teenager.

Teenagers aren't as bad as they're made out to be. **They're about 55 times feckin' worse.** They're these noisy, hungry, misshapen things, erupting suddenly with great clumps of hair, shambling around, trying to bag anything with a pulse. Jaysus, they're like horny werewolves.

You can't stop teenagers experimenting – with smoking, drinking, not paying for stuff, you know the sort of thing. It's a big old world they're gearing up for, and they're programmed to try things out. But hopefully not on your best couch without putting down a feckin' towel first.

It's worth learning a few of Mammy's tips for dealing with their little excursions up Pain-In-The-Arse Street.

1 Smoking

Most of my lot tried smoking at least once. It breaks a mother's heart to see them poisoning themselves when you've treated their bodies as little temples, never feeding them so much as a leftover sausage without scraping the fur off first.

But I couldn't just say 'stop' to them, could I? I used to smoke more than the John West factory. When you've done forty a day, you can't take the moral high ground. You can't take any high ground. Your lungs'd feckin' burst.

So I got clever. I had some ashtrays made with my face at the bottom of them. I thought, they'll never stub their butts on their dear old Mammy, will they? Of course they didn't. They stubbed them out in the bucking plant pots instead. That aspidistra was a cutting from my great-great-grandmammy's one. Four generations it survived, and it was killed by passive smoking.

If you can't beat them, join them. Buy them some smokes. A little trip to the docks and a word in the right shell can sort you out with a packet of vicious Turkish fags. You might not recognize the brand, but get the ones that smell like camel: not the cigarette brand, the animal. The one that shits on burning hot sand. That sort of smell. A quick wheeze on one of those and they'll be coughing hard enough to ralph up an eye and swearing they'll never touch another.

❷ *Drinking*

Lock your drinks cabinet. They can find their own feckin' booze. And it might not be a certificate in chartered accountancy, but there's always work for someone who can crack a padlock.

Then all you have to worry about is the drugs. Heron. Maharajahuana. All that cocaine they shove up each other's arses in the rock bands in the Sunday papers, like you wouldn't believe. They're all doing it. It wasn't like that in my day, back in the Sixties.

Jaysus. I don't like to even think about someone in my family doing drugs. I'll have one of my turns and have to neck a handful of feckin' pills. I don't know what the world's coming to, I really feckin' don't.

❸ *S-E-K-S*

As long as they're not ramming it down each other's throats, I don't mind what they get up to.

❹ *Contraception*

Now, I know Father Quinn won't agree with me, but I say there's nothing wrong with a man wearing a diving suit if he's exploring uncharted depths. The last thing anyone wants down there is a surprise, especially a nasty one, like crabs or octopuses.

I say take precautions. Well, multiple births run in my family. I put a rubber mat in the bath to avoid unwanted slip-ups, and I see no difference when it comes to keeping the family at a manageable size *(rugby team or thereabouts)*.

⑤ Trouble with the Law

Time was when any rascal getting up to mischief got a thick ear from the local copper. But they have to fill in five different forms now before they can give kids a thick ear, so Buster says.

Your teenager's going to have a run-in with the law eventually, unless they're one of those angelic little bollix that wins Young Musician of the Year. Weird little feckers, shut in a room playing with themselves, fiddling away all day and night, pounding away at their organ, running their fingers up and down their oboe till their hands are red raw. What sort of life's that for a teenage boy?

It's worth drumming into them at an early age the difference between right, wrong and getting away with it.

⑥ Music

Sooner or later you'll hear a rhythmic thumping on the floorboards from your little angel's bedroom. You worry they're having S-E-K-S, but it's worse than that.

They've discovered 'music'. Well, they call it music. There's music and there's music. And there's also people shouting their own names over what sounds like a three-armed drummer getting electrocuted in a shipping container. That's not music. At best, it's showing off. At worst, it's torture. Either way, it's what headphones were invented for.

So, say they find a purse on the street. There's three ways of dealing with it:

RIGHT

Handing it in to the police with a smile like butter wouldn't melt in your darling little mouth.

WRONG

Emptying it and dropping it back in the street. That's littering, and you could get fined for that.

GETTING AWAY WITH IT

Handing it in to the police €10 lighter. Time is money, and you always have to queue at the police station.

MAMMY'S TIP

Carry a trumpet with you on the bus. If one of the horny werewolves starts playing their 'music' out loud on their phone, take your trumpet out and blow it into their ear. And say, 'Mind if I play along? I love this one!'

❼ Driving Lessons

Our Dermot could drive before he could talk. Though he was past getting away with that excuse when he was pulled over on his mobile. I kept blaming myself for giving a phone to a thirteen-year-old. Then I realized I hadn't. I still don't know where he got it. Or the car.

Children's parties

Kiddies' parties can be a right pain in the arse. When my Dermot turned four, Billy O'Reilly came and did a few tricks. Mainly making the kids disappear when he arrived in his homemade clown make-up. Face like a frightened pizza. The poor kiddies nearly shit themselves. I told Billy he should have used a mirror.

 The secret to a kiddies' party is in the preparation. A pint of Whiskey Mac in a Tizer bottle under the sink can make the difference between three hours with your hands over your ears trying to wrangle a stampede in a feckin' abattoir and a perfectly bearable afternoon. Here are some little things you can rustle up beforehand to make a truly magical day for your little angel.

FOOD

Cheesy Wotsits are always a winner. And they're mainly air, so the little ones won't get full up. Then they'll eat the sandwiches. Someone's got to eat the sandwiches. No grown-up wants that much feckin' jam.

Cocktail sausages. The little mini ones. (Sure, I've never known why they're called cocktail sausages. What kind of bollix has a sausage in his gin?) If you can't find cocktail sausages, get the ordinary ones and cook them twice as long. You'll get more shrinkage than Grandad in a cold bath.

Jelly. You've got to have jelly. Kids love jelly. It's food (I think) and it wobbles. Anything that wobbles keeps kids happy. (In fact, I can think of plenty of grown-ups who can be kept happy watching stuff wobble. Beach feckin' volleyball, they call it.) Plus you can hide things in jelly: little sweeties and that. Not Cheesy Wotsits, though. Winnie tried that once. Father Quinn says it's the only wake he's ever been sick at.

Squash. The kiddies love squash. And if it's running a bit low, add some food colouring and dilute it a bit more. I've made a bottle last three birthdays like that.

Birthday cake. Something in a funny shape. Hedgehog's a nice easy one. Swiss roll with a load of matches in it. Though take the battery out of the smoke alarm before you pop the candles in.

GAMES

Pass the parcel. Easy. A Chocolate Kimberley wrapped in newspaper inside a Chocolate Kimberley wrapped in newspaper inside a Chocolate Kimberley wrapped in newspaper inside a Chocolate Kimberley wrapped in newspaper inside a Chocolate Kimberley wrapped in newspaper and so on. The only thing is the fecker takes about a fortnight to get ready and if there's more than about a dozen kiddies coming to the party you end up with something the size of a rolled-up duvet and you've done the budgie out of a year's worth of carpet.

Musical chairs. You need plenty of chairs for this to work. If you haven't got enough, try musical stairs. You might get a few tumbles and scrapes, but it gets the party over quicker.

Dead lions. The kiddies have to lie perfectly still for as long as they can. The first one to move has to go and get the grown-ups back from the pub in time to dish out the prizes to the winners.

GOODIE BAGS

Don't forget the goodie bags. A Chocolate Kimberley, a slice of hedgehog and a deflated sea giraffe are usually enough. And in case one of the kiddies is a pain in the arse, make up a baddie bag with a few doggie choc drops in it. That'll teach the little fecker. They taste worse than the inside of a gardening glove.

PLUS DOGGIE CHOC DROPS

Balloon animals

Balloon animals. Always a hit. You think there's something hard about making balloon animals? Is there feck. Here's a few easy ones.

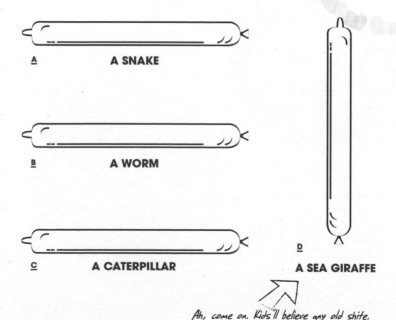

A   **A SNAKE**

B   **A WORM**

C   **A CATERPILLAR**

D

A SEA GIRAFFE

Ah, come on. Kids'll believe any old shite.

Ah, what is love? Many have tried to answer that question.

Love is all you need

Is it bollix. Try paying a gas bill with a kiss.

Love is the Tender Trap

No. That's zipping up your flies too fast.

Love is All Around

You're thinking of dogshit.

LOVE IS THE SWEETEST THING

Sweeter than builder's tea? You must be joking.

So what is it? Ah, I don't feckin' know.

But love is what holds a family together. When you're under each other's feet, driving each other to distraction, what's the one thing that stops you going at your nearest and dearest with bits of broken furniture?

Love.

That, and the laws against aggravated bodily harm. But mainly love.

And the love that holds a family together started as the love between two people. Two people who decided to join up, and make more people. I tell you, apart from that chocolate stuff you put on ice cream that goes hard, is there anything in this world more magical?

THE BIRDS AND THE BEES

You might dread the day, but sure enough, your children will turn to you for advice on, shall we say, bedroom matters, and I'm not talking about choosing a valance. Tough. Even if you don't want to give them advice straight, you're the example they've grown up with, so they'll be following in your footsteps whatever. Face it. They're feckin' screwed.

They'll only hear terrible things about S-E-K-S behind the bike sheds. If I still believed what I heard in the playground about how a man and a woman make a baby, I wouldn't have any kids, I'll tell you that, but I'd have a feckin' huge belly button.

What they need is honest and clear advice from someone who knows. You.

So how do you tell them about the birds and the bees? Well, you don't want to frighten them – there's such a thing as too much too young (I've never forgiven myself for leaving that drawing Redser did where little Trevor could find it) – so choose what you tell them when.

Be My Valentine

Here's what to say:

Mammy, where do babies come from?

UNDER 5

Feck off and pick up your Stickle Bricks.

Mammy, did the stork bring me?

5–8 YEARS OLD

Feck off and pick up your Lego.

Mammy, Clare at school says babies come out your bum.

8–11 YEARS OLD

Feck off and pick up your bike.

Mammy, can someone have a baby if they sit on a warm toilet seat?

11–15 YEARS OLD

Feck off and pick up your fags before your father sees.

Mammy, I think I might have got a girl pregnant.

15–18 YEARS OLD

For feck's sake, how did that happen? Don't you listen to a word I feckin' say?

18+

Mammy, where do babies come from?

Aw, will you feck off and make sure Buster's learned his speech? It's your wedding, it's up to you if you want to ruin it.

GETTING SHOT OF YOUR CHILDREN

So you've given them all the tools they need to make it in the world of love, but still every morning there's that telltale extra cereal bowl left nowhere near the feckin' sink. Your kid's still under your roof. And that's not natural.

One thing I've learned? They all take their own sweet time. You have to be patient. But it can be hard. You've got a child who you know is ready to fly, but you can't seem to pair them off. It breaks your heart. They're the apple of your eye. Why won't anyone take a feckin' bite?

Chances are they're underselling themselves. It's fair enough; I remember **Dermot** found it very uncomfortable blowing his own trumpet. He couldn't do it, and not for lack of trying. I could hear him through his bedroom door every night, crying with frustration. Which is why I'm delighted that he's got **Maria** now, to blow it for him.

Mark and **Betty**, now, were no trouble. He knew what he wanted. He's a good practical boy. And though she can be feisty, I respect that, and I know they're happy together. Well, she tells me so, and I've never heard him disagree.

Give them time. They'll find their own sweet way.

It used to drive me mad, how **Rory** could never seem to meet the right girl. But now I know if I'd hurried him, he'd have ended up married to that boss-eyed girl from the nail bar. And then he'd never have found **Dino**. Turns out we were all looking in the wrong place. And so was she.

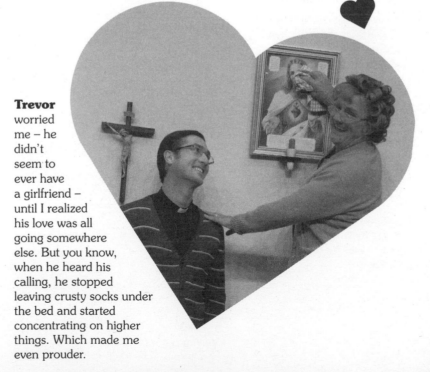

Trevor worried me – he didn't seem to ever have a girlfriend – until I realized his love was all going somewhere else. But you know, when he heard his calling, he stopped leaving crusty socks under the bed and started concentrating on higher things. Which made me even prouder.

Cathy had a terrible time of it as a teenager, bringing home some right shockers. The ones with brains had no looks and the ones with looks had no brains. I don't know how some of them kept moving around. I came up with a vetting system. I asked them a simple question – 'How are ye doing?' – and if they didn't know the answer, they weren't allowed on the soft furniture.

We made a list once of all Cathy's men, and what the problem was, to try to see a pattern:

Dean – too hairy

Alan – too short

Kenny – too hairy and short

Ricky – hair too short

Marko – obsessed with
          Daniel O'Donnell

Lee – only talked about football

Damien – never talked about
            football (suspicious)

Niall – no eyebrows

Stevo – kept sneezing

Bryan – tiny ears, big face

Pete – punched waiter and ran

Mickey – dogskin coat

Robbie – musical

Dr Lucas – punched me and ran

Tony – sick in handbag (own)

The pattern was clear. Cathy was too fussy.

But every time she brought someone new home, I thought, '**Fuck me, you've not been fussy enough, my girl**.'

There are a lot of weird, untrustworthy men out there. I know. I married one, God rest his sweet memory.

But Cathy's my only daughter, for feck's sake. I don't want her spending a hopeless fortnight trying to make it work with some dirty-fingernailed oaf with alopecia and a wharfinger's tongue who'll lie about stealing her knickers to sell to the dossers slumped round the newspaper racks down the library in exchange for baccy and pills. Not twice, anyway.

Anyway, Cathy said she'd try internet dating. I tried to put her off. Trusting a computer to guide you in the ways of love? You'll end up being matched with a feckin' speak-your-weight machine.

What does an internet know about the bond between a man and a woman? Even if times are hard, even if he's a bum, you still love that man of yours. Those words would mean nothing to an internet. Trust me. Go to your internet now, and type in HARD BUM LOVE. I tell you, you'll get nothing.

Anyway, she didn't listen and she went onto one of those electric dating sites on her computer, and while she was in the toilet, I filled it in for her and pressed 'close' to send it off, like you do. She'll be beating off perfect men with a shitty stick, I feckin' tell you.

Do it. After all, who knows your little darling better than you do?

EVERYDAY to LOVER

Name: Catherine Brown   Se 21   F

Looking for:

A nice young man

Interests:

Long walks, being bought stuff, none of that

Describe your ideal partner:

Lapsed priest, but not for anything
perverted or stealing money

Rate the following 5 characteristics of a potential
partner in order of importance (1=high, 5=lower):

1 Good looks

1 Good job/job prospects

1 Good sense of humour

1 Good personal hygiene

1 Good moral values

Other:

Yes. All of these. And a car with four doors

Are you looking for a long-term relationship?

Yes and grandchildren

Do you believe in love at first sight?

No. Second opinion required 081 106 6090 (Agnes)

Religious background:

Catholic

Is religion important to you?

Prepared to change to anything except
Scientangelist or suicide bomber

Do you like to travel?

Yes but allergic to bus/coach.
Car with four doors preferred

Where do you see yourself in five years' time?

School open day

Submit

WOOING

I remember my first date with Redser. Well, one of us had to. He was so nervous he'd given himself a double dose of Dutch courage before I arrived. I remember his first words to me: 'I'm down here.' And the moment our eyes met under the table.

But that man, with his red-rimmed eyes and his one shoe, was the man I was to spend my life with, the one who'd make a new centre for my universe, by giving me either six or seven wonderful children. I forget which. Then nature took its course, as it always does, and from that unpromising acorn, a beautiful willow tree grew.

From my position (the missionary), love looks so much simpler than it does to my kids. They seem so fragile at times, my lot – frightened that a spat with their other half means the relationship is over. Honestly. If I'd let a little barney rattle me, my kids wouldn't be here. But I wouldn't let Little Barney rattle me, and so he ran away with that barmaid, and I had to settle for Redser.

But then my kids are all just starting out on the race of life. I'm almost at the finish line, looking back over my shoulder, like Usain Bolt, wondering how I got here so feckin' fast.

No, not the finish line. I'm not planning on clocking off before Grandad. I want to cash all that goodwill in first. Let's say I'm looking at them all from a bench. At the side. Coaching. I suppose that's what this book is.

So, as a coach, what's the one piece of advice I'd give about love?

It's this – **Don't listen to my advice**.

Nobody should tell anybody else how to find love, or to keep love. That's something only you can work out for yourself.

All the theory in the world doesn't beat hands-on practice. Though if you let too many people practise putting their hands on you, you can get yourself a reputation. Poor Molly Nolan. She swears to this day it was a life-modelling class for art students who were blind.

It's not my business to tell others how to live their lives. Which is why I've kept that to a minimum in this book I've been asked to write about life advice. Stuff it. They can't have the money back. I cashed the cheque. It's gone.

LOVE AT FIRST SIGHT

In books and films, people
fall in love at just a glance.
But what does a glance tell
you about someone? That
they've brushed their hair?
That they know which
way round to button their
cardigan *(buttons at the
front)*? You're in for a lot of
disappointment if you expect
them to look as good for the
rest of your lives together as
they did in that one moment
where your eyes first met.
Now I look back, I see Redser
really let himself go after that
first date. It was the last time
I ever saw him in socks.

So I've tried not to comment
on the fearful bog-creatures
my lot have dragged home
over the years, even if I can
read the warning signs. I
remember Cathy turning up
with a very unsuitable young
man, all tattoos up his neck
and a flick-knife scar. But I
knew I had to let it take its
natural course. After all,
it's what he has inside that
counts. And, sure enough, it
turned out he had three years
inside. For stealing a cement
mixer. When she found
out, she dropped him like a
burning shit.

WARNING SIGNS

With luck, you'll find the perfect match. Just be prepared to kiss a few ugly frogs on your long journey to find that handsome ~~fro~~prince. And remember: there's no point flogging a dead horse, unless you're Billy Knock's abattoir. Sometimes that spark isn't there.

Ask yourself the following questions:

🦠 If they're reading *The Racing Post* when you arrive, do they keep reading it while you're talking?

🦠 Do they make you pay for dinner up front and then ask you to leave so they can eat it undisturbed?

🦠 Do they refer to you by your gender instead of your name? 'You, woman.'

🦠 Do they refuse to make eye contact at dinner? Are their eyes closed? Is there snoring?

🦠 After you turn the lights down low, do they noisily snap on a pair of rubber gloves before starting foreplay?

🦠 Have they ever sent a friend or relative in their place?

🦠 Have they ever asked you to send a friend or relative in your place?

If you answered yes to any of these, they are warning signs that your date isn't that interested.

Most importantly, be yourself. I said as much to himself myself. Don't be selfish, but let your inner self be your outer self and you'll be self-confidence itself. Not an off-the-shelf self, but your own true self itself. That should be self-evident.

There's no point hiding anything, because they'll find out in the end. You know the story of Cyrano de Bergerac? He got someone else to woo his lady for him, and when she found out he was bullshitting, he ran away to the Channel Islands and became a feckin' policeman. Nobody wants that.

But if the chemistry's there, all this romance only leads to one thing. I don't want to spell it out, but it starts with an S, and ends with an S, and there's a K in the middle. And I don't mean scissor-kicks.

THE TEN COMMANDMENTS OF
SEX

1. If you wouldn't put it in your mouth, don't put it anywhere near your whatsit.

2. Thongs are what people with lisps sing. A string with a bit of bunting sewn to it is no way of keeping your bits warm. You might as well put a necklace round your waist and stick a Dairylea wrapper to it.

3. Never go the whole way on a first date. Or at least until he's been to the bar. And don't ask about nuts. It'll only get him going.

4. Tell him: if he likes you, he'll wait for you. If he says you're like a nice wine or a spring flower, he might be full of shite but at least he's trying. If he says you're like a bus, tell him you're not going his way and besides, you don't come that often.

5. He's got to make an effort. If he doesn't turn up for the first three dates, don't go on a fourth with him. It'll only end in tears.

6. Take it one step at a time. If he wants to skip to the bit where he falls asleep before he's done the other bits, bin the fecker.

7. Don't let him talk you into anything you're not happy with. Like the shed. There are far warmer places you can go.

8. If he asks you to put something on to get him going, that's fine. Unless it's a Corrs album.

9. Don't be afraid to try something new. Except the shed. Even if it's a new shed.

10. Sex is all about trust. If you can't have sex with him, don't expect to be able to trust him.

WHAT NOW?

So you've found the right person, and you know what bit goes where and for how long and what'll happen if you get it right.

NOW SLOW DOWN. THINK.
WHERE IS THIS ALL HEADING?

Imagine the scene. You're lying in bed in the small hours of the morning. The one you love is by your side. It's been a full night of lovemaking and you've been thrusting away like a feckin' porn star for the past four, five, even six minutes. Now roll over and look at the person you're with. There they are. Musky. Perhaps steaming slightly.

Now imagine it's twenty-five years on. You're still here, in the same position. In the half-dark. Awake, close and whispering.

Can you imagine that? Twenty-five years.

Then imagine you're really awake because there's a babby screaming like the four-minute warning, and you've not properly touched each other except by mistake for two decades because you're so tired you're practically transparent. The last time you had any time to yourselves was when the lock jammed in the bathroom that time he was having a shit and you'd come in for the nappy cream.

Hold that thought. It's the best contraception there is.

As I always yell through the letterbox at any of my lot when they head out on a first date: multiple births run in this family. So you need to think before you... and that means contraception.

CONTRACEPTION

No beating around the bush (and that's a pretty good piece of contraception advice right there), to my mind, contraception is like the bit where Sinatra stops the band and chats to the audience: it's time for frank talking.

Some parents don't like to discuss these sorts of downstairs affairs with their children. But you have to make sure your kids know what the options are so they can forget them, just like you did, which is why you're having this conversation at all.

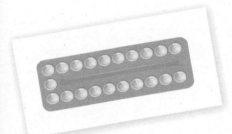

THE PILL
Doesn't feckin' work. As soon as you stand up, it falls out.

CONDOM
Against God himself, if you believe in that sort of thing. Also if your man gets as hot as Redser did on the approach, you get a smell of burning rubber like a tyre-yard fire, and that's a terrible turn-off. So, actually, surprisingly effective.

CAP
Has to be fitted by an expert. I never really liked the idea of having someone else in the bedroom. I imagine it puts you right off your stroke. Effective.

COIL

The more copper in your coil, the more effective it is, but there's an increased risk of getting the piping swiped out of your knickers while you're slumped drunk under a table by some passing scrutter with an eye on the scrap market. Fit a padlock.

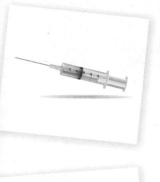

INJECTION

Can't see how one more prick's going to undo the damage. Two wrongs don't make a right.

RHYTHM METHOD

You need to be able to plan this on the calendar, and mine's a bit of a jumble. Found out I was timing myself to hairdressing appointments, and that explains Trevor.

FEMIDOM

Plastic bag to pick up a dog turd – and makes the same noise, so extremely off-putting for both of you. Very effective.

Let's face it. You're going to end up pregnant.

WHAT TO EXPECT
WHEN YOU'RE FECKIN' EXPECTING

These days, you can hardly move for pregnancy advice. Have you been in a bookshop lately? I went in with Dermot and Maria when she was up the duff, and there's three walls of books about expecting. *I wasn't feckin' expecting that.*

Mammy's Tip

Are those old drawers getti[ng] a bit stubborn? Loosen the[m] up by rubbing a bar of so[ap] along the gusset.

The Pregnancy Bible. The Rough Guide to Pregnancy. Your Pregnancy Week by Week. Your Pregnancy Day by Day. Your Pregnancy Minute by Feckin' Minute. There was probably a Haynes manual and a pop-up book in there somewhere too.

There's even books for men. Like they do anything at all, apart from get you in that state in the first place. It's like a bucking hit and run: *'Did you see what hit you?'* *'No, the lights were off . . .'*

There wasn't any of that nonsense when I had our Mark. If I'd gone into the library and asked for some help with pregnancy back then, Sweaty Cormac would have chased me out of the building with an oversized hardback.

The other thing is that pregnancy isn't conducted in English any more. It's all foreign now. When Maria was expecting the boys, it was all 'trimester' this and 'lanugo' that and, honestly, I needed a feckin' Pregnancy–English dictionary to translate it. I thought meconium was a sort of pasta. And I could have sworn the colostrum was one of them big theatres.

Follow their advice and you'd never eat either. They've taken every honest-to-feckin'-goodness food stuff and put it on a prohibition list. They have you practically living off pills. It's like being a feckin' astronaut. Maria had vitamins, Evening Primrose oil (which she used to take in the mornings, so it probably didn't work anyway) and something called follicle acid, which is what stops broccoli growing hair.

It's all because nobody asks their feckin' Mammy any more, that's what it is. But who'll give it to you straight, without any beating around the bush? *(Which is where the feckin' problem begins, and you bucking know it.)* Who's not going to pull any punches?

Mammy.

CONCEPTION

Some people find it embarrassing telling their kids where babies come from. But all it takes is honesty. Look into their eyes and say, 'When a Mammy and a daddy love each other very much, they do a special love dance. Look I'll show you. Hold my tea, I need to get my knickers down. Where are you going? Come back!' And that way they can find out the gory details from the dirty kids behind the bike sheds, the way nature feckin' intended.

FINDING OUT YOU'RE WITH CHILD

Well, obviously, there's the telltale signs. Like being able to afford more food because you've stopped spending a feckin' fortune on women's toiletries. Jaysus, it costs a fortune just keeping yourself decent. I think it was when Redser saw what it ate out of the household budget keeping me in monthly necessaries that he decided to have six kids. Me being pregnant saved enough in ten years for him to make some serious investments in the bloodstock industry. And then watch them come in fourth. The daft bollix.

You can buy those little thermometers you have to widdle on, but they're about €10 each. That's a lot of money for something you were only planning on spending a penny on. And some of them have got digital watches and calculators and feck knows what else built into them now. You wouldn't catch me peeing on a digital watch.

The thing is, if you've a bun in the oven, you'll know soon enough when it starts to rise. You'll feel that indescribable bloom. How to describe that indescribable feeling?

Knackered. That's it. Feckin' knackered.

BEING FECKIN' KNACKERED

Jaysus, if pregnancy doesn't take the wind out of your sails. Some mornings I woke up feeling like I'd pushed a piano up a feckin' mountain in my sleep. The only reason to get out of bed was so I could have a sit down.

Of course, it's Mother Nature's way of preparing you for the feckin' sledgehammering you're going to get once your little bundle of joy comes out and needs full-time attention for the first thirty or forty years.

CRAVINGS

Cravings are a funny thing. You're eating for two, and the shite you're eating is off the feckin' scale.

They say if you're craving sweet things, it's a girl, and if it's salty things, it's a boy. What a load of shite. Every woman who ever lived craved chocolate and as far as I can feckin' tell, there's still plenty of boys being born.

Besides, there's a whole shiteload of these old wives' tales. If you've heartburn, it's a boy. If you sleep on your right, it's a girl. If you've cold feet – well, if you've cold feet, it's no feckin' surprise. No woman ever got through her first pregnancy without looking down the settee at himself, picking his feet with the bottle opener, and thinking, *'How the living shite is that lazy feckin' eejit going to be a father?'*

I had some pretty odd cravings. With Mark, it was tarmac. Not to eat. Just the smell. Didn't I wander the streets looking for roadworks, just to get a whiff of the stuff? 'What'd you do today?' Redser would ask. 'Watched some fellows digging a hole in the road,' I'd say. 'Was there nothing better on the TV?' he'd say.

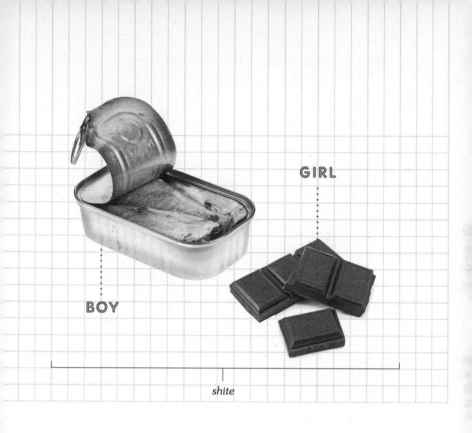

GIRL

BOY

shite

With Rory, it was lettuce. I was munching through so much of the stuff, Redser offered to build me a hutch.

With Cathy, it was chlorine, so I did a lot of standing by the vents outside the swimming baths. Kept me nice and warm, but I smelled like a lifeguard's laundry basket when I got home.

It was chips with Dermot.

Redser was feckin' delighted. After the first week of having chips for dinner every night, he said he thought we ought to have another twenty kids.

MORNING SICKNESS

I never had the morning sickness until Dermot. But it could have been all the chips the night before, I suppose. Winnie had it rotten with Sharon. She spent half her time in the bathroom throwing up, and the other half in the bathroom cleaning it off. Mind you, you've never seen such a spotless pan. She could have eaten her dinner off it, except she was too busy doing the reverse.

Now, it's nice to have that bump to begin with. All the fluttering and kicking, it's like having a starling trapped in a flue. Except then it turns into a feckin' vulture. A vulture in steel-capped boots.

And then there's everybody rubbing it. I might as well have been a feckin' genie's lamp when I had Mark. Wore a hole in my best cardigan, it did.

As for the weight – don't expect to do the stairs in a hurry after the first few months. By the time it's halfway grown, you already feel like you've swallowed a bowling ball. Come the end of the pregnancy, it's like you're smuggling a spacehopper full of concrete. And then you've got to shit that thing out.

Dermot was 13lb 7oz when he was born. He tore the arse out of me. I had more stitches than Frankenstein's feckin' monster. I couldn't look down there for weeks, and when I did, Jaysus! I've seen better laced football boots.

The midwife asked me right after if I'd like a cup of tea. I said I was worried it might come straight back out the other end. I didn't dare sneeze for the first year after Dermot was born, in case I ruined a pair of shoes.

Redser wasn't keen on being down the business end for the birth, so he went to the pub instead. He said it was a da's duty to wet the babby's head. I told him I thought he ought to see the head first. He said, *'Sure, I've the rest of my life to look at the babby's head, but the pub shuts at midnight.'*

THE BIRTH

Put it this way: you can either have the babby at home, in comfort, like all mammies have done for thousands of feckin' years, or you can have it in a steaming hot room under scorching striplights, surrounded by tubes and machines and people in wipe-clean uniforms. You might as well give birth in the boiler room of a feckin' power station.

It's not the most relaxing situation to bring a baby into the world, but then neither's the back of an ice cream van on bank holiday weekend, and Winnie's Mammy managed that. Sometimes you have to make the best of what you've got. Winnie's da made a feckin' 99.

A lot of people want it as nature intended, and who can blame them? They want it – what do they call it? Organic. What the French call O'Natrel. They don't want the first thing the kiddie sees to be a wall-mounted canister of antibacterial handwash and a feckin' anaesthetist. Fair enough. The little mites weren't conceived in a spotless, clinical environment. Well, Dermot's Maria probably was. I'll bet her Mammy washes the gravel on her feckin' drive and triple-folds her toilet roll to avoid finger-through. The way she looks at my feckin' kitchen overflow, you'd think she'd never poked spaghetti hoops down hers.

They have all these new births you can do now, like water births. Fine, if you like it, but I can't swim, and I can't believe they do a rubber ring that'd fit round a bump like Dermot. There are feckin' ring roads that wouldn't have got round that.

When Mark and Betty had Bono, they had this birth plan they'd worked out. The stuff they wanted to bring with them, they should have hired feckin' Sherpas. They're very organized people. Mark's very sensible, very precise. He used to do his colouring books one pen at a time, all the reds on all the pages, then all the blues. I always knew he'd grow up to do something with his hands, but I was worried it would be serial killing.

I couldn't believe how much they'd planned it out. Pages and pages of the stuff. The whole birth broken down, with everything written out – pain relief, where they'd be, who'd be screaming.

It was like the script to a feckin' play. A nativity play, I suppose.

And you know what a nativity play is like.

Everyone's watching, then your kid comes out unexpectedly, at the wrong time, facing the wrong way and refuses to make a feckin' sound for two minutes. And when someone grabs the babby and holds it up, it looks like a doll, and everyone's got tears in their eyes, and suddenly the kid's crying too, but then you realize that this – all the chaos and surprise and willing everybody on – is what it all means, what we're all here for, and there's something magic in all the mess.

That's what birth's like. It's magic. And, as always happens in magic, the woman ends up getting split in feckin' half.

GETTING SPLIT IN FECKIN' HALF

It's a Mammy's job to pass on the truth about the joy of childbirth to the younger generation. *And the only reason there are any more children is that it's the younger generation's job to think she's exaggerating.*

Jaysus. I tell you. There are these midwives and nurses down your sharp end, yelling at you to 'push', and you're thinking, *'No, you push, either side of me, or I'm going to break in feckin' two.'*

You start to wish you were one of those snakes with detachable parts that can get an antelope through. If we're made in God's image, it's no feckin' wonder he made someone else give birth to his son. It's the wrong feckin' shape down there, and he feckin' knows it.

If you've ever tried to post a watermelon through a letterbox, you'll have some idea. Believe me, I've done it plenty, and every time, it's like shitting a bike.

LETTER BOX

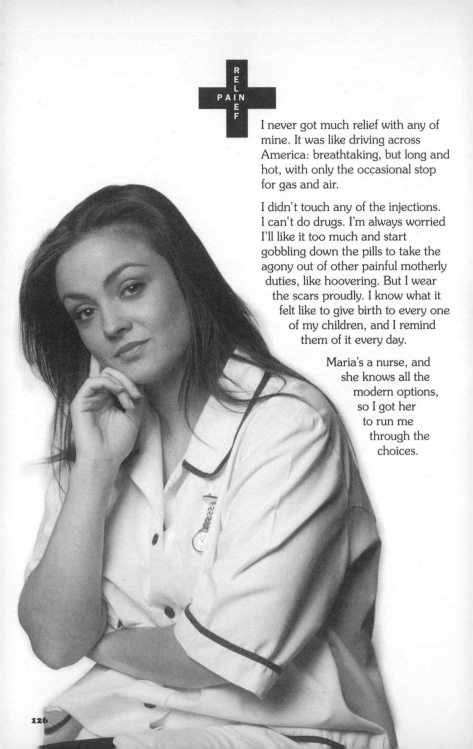

R
E
L
PAIN **I**
E
F

I never got much relief with any of mine. It was like driving across America: breathtaking, but long and hot, with only the occasional stop for gas and air.

I didn't touch any of the injections. I can't do drugs. I'm always worried I'll like it too much and start gobbling down the pills to take the agony out of other painful motherly duties, like hoovering. But I wear the scars proudly. I know what it felt like to give birth to every one of my children, and I remind them of it every day.

Maria's a nurse, and she knows all the modern options, so I got her to run me through the choices.

GAS AND AIR

Effect: Reduces pain, can cause laughter.

Notes: Works. Good basic pain control.

PETHIDINE / DIAMORPHINE

Effect: Morphine-like woozy numbness.

Notes: Works, but can make your baby want to steal people's car stereos.

EPIDURAL

Effect: Total blocking of pain.

Notes: Works, but you're not really there. Which, if you're having triplets, like I did, is exactly where you want to be.

TENS MACHINE

Effect: Fiddly electric-pulse thingy you operate yourself.

Notes: <u>Doesn't work</u>. Or rather, it might work if trying to remember the instructions at the same time as giving birth wasn't like making a prizewinning soufflé during a plane crash.

HOMEOPATHY & HYPNOSIS

Effect: Annoys the nurses.

Notes: <u>Doesn't work</u>.

OTHER THINGS THAT DON'T WORK:

- Holding your breath

- Humming

- Laughing

- Pressing a fishfinger against the affected area like when you pierce your ears

- Writing to your MEP demanding immediate action

THINGS THAT DO WORK:

- Keeping your legs together nine months earlier

C-SECTION

By choice or by chance you may
end up going for a local anaesthetic
and having them take the baby
out the sun-roof. But you won't
be hula-hooping for months. Plus,
Buster Brady was born that way and
he has a proper awful tendency to
nip in and out of houses through the
window without the owners knowing
what's going on. I reckon he got the
idea really early on.

AFTER THE BIRTH

There's all sorts of stuff that happens after
the birth. Stuff you don't want to read about,
take it from me. Let's just say it can take
an expert to get the curtains closed. And it
might be a while before you'll be wanting
to let any daylight back in. Or anything else,
for that matter.

Mammy's Tip

*Prevent your best plates from
becoming chipped or scratched by
not having any
feckin' children. Alternatively,
don't have any best plates.*

Baby names

So what are you going to call your babby? Have you seen the things people call their kids these days? I had a quick look at the births section in the paper, and I couldn't believe my eyes.

B
A
B
Y

Manhattanna
Bisto-Luke
Moog
Omelette
Prosecco
Alcopop

Pussy-Jo
Toilettina
Shergar
Humvee
Ketamine

What the feck? Those aren't names. They're bad hands in feckin' Scrabble.

A baby should be named after a saint. A saint's name is dignified and traditional. And there are plenty to choose from. Why not give your babby the best start in life with one of these?

The last thing you want is to have them bullied at school. Don't forget: at some point, your little sweetheart is going to turn around and blame you for everything bad in their life. Don't give them a feckin' reason on day one.

B
A
B
Y

Brinolph
Poppo
Branvalator
Gay
Mocheomoc
Frumence

Godehard
Wigbert
Radbod
Sexburgis
Leopard

Grandchildren

From the moment you become a Mammy, your life seems to go faster and faster. I suppose everything goes faster when it's going downhill. All that joy and all those tears, whipping by like the view out of the window of a runaway train. It seems only five minutes ago that I was mopping arses, mashing up food and wondering would it ever end. But then I think, Grandad'll die soon, and I'll probably miss him.

Anyway, before you know it, your babies have had babies. I didn't see that coming. Jaysus. Talk about an eye opener. I'm a feckin' grandmother. I was always a grand mother, but . . . you know. A granny? Hard to believe to look at me, with my model figure and zest for life, but I'm a Mammy to some daddies.

Seriously, it's been wonderful. If a child is the greatest gift of all, then I can only say that a grandchild is a greatester one. The true blessing of being a grandparent is you get to enjoy the whole thing again, but you sleep through bits of it this time.

You'll be called on for advice, you'll be asked to look after them, but you get to give them back afterwards because they're too wee to take down the feckin' bingo. It's a win-win. And if you win at the bingo, it's a win-win-win.

Best of all you'll get to tell them all sorts of shite, and they'll believe you. Let their parents deal with the consequences. You're Granny (or Grandad). Abuse your position.

Lies to tell grandchildren

Your hair grows towards the moon.

Ostriches can spin webs.

You've got four cheeks on your body: two on your face and two on your feet.

Policemen keep free toys under their hats.

If you step on the cracks in the pavement, the council will eat you.

People on the equator can sneeze rainbows.

Speed humps are where dinosaurs are buried.

If you don't brush your teeth you'll grow grass on your face.

The tomato is really a fish.

Father Christmas is 817 years old. If you don't send him a birthday card, you get dung for Christmas.

If you leave an onion under your pillow, the onion fairy will give you money.

There's no such word as 'feck'.

Jesus was Irish.

That's not how Old Mr Feenan went blind, so stop saying it.

If you swallow that chewing gum you'll turn into a spacehopper.

It takes 45 muscles to frown, but none to look bored. So make a feckin' effort.

They're not vegetables, they're green sweeties.

You're adopted.

SEX AND THE OLDER WOMAN

Some people (not me) who are old enough to be grandparents may not seem as attractive any more, so they (not me) get ignored, but they're human beings, with needs. And they (not me) should have something to get them through the day.

It might not be very dignified to talk about it, but as an old person's body ages, they can find certain urges quite difficult to control. Take Winnie. Many times she's gone home after a cup and a chat, and I've found she's left something mucky behind on one of my kitchen chairs. I'm fairly broadminded, but believe me, there are times I've not wanted to pick it up.

I'm talking about saucy books.

Now, you wouldn't know it to look at her, but Winnie is a devil for triple-X smut. It's where she gets her kicks. Me, I'm not a big reader of blue books, but if nobody's about, I'll grab whatever racy paperback Winnie's left behind and have a quick flick myself. I like to have a bit of a thumb for a few minutes, until I've come to my own conclusions. Just a swift riffle, you know, purely for my own pleasure. I'm only human.

You'd be surprised. They're good, some of them. It's not all pump-pump-squirt. It's quite sweet, bits of it. Not like the shocking magazines under Dermot's bed. Jaysus, the last one I pulled out looked like a seafood catalogue, and didn't smell much better. Winnie's stuff is what they call 'eurotica'. I think it's what they call porn now we're in the Euro. I preferred it when it was Punts. **You knew where you stood with a Punt. Plus, it rhymed with bank manager.**

Eurotica is all about the imagination. It's what you don't see, not what you do see. And I tell you, you don't see much with a feckin' bag over your head, handcuffed buck-naked to a filing cabinet, like the poor woman in the one Winnie left behind last week.

Here are some of Winnie's books I've enjoyed having a good skim through. Who knows? You might too!

TREAT YOURSELF TO SEX

PLOT: Not much of a story, this one, just instructions, like you get with flatpack furniture: it looks like a devil of a lot of screwing and the more I look at the diagram, the more I worry I've been given the wrong parts. They try it all ways, and it's a bit repetitive. I don't know if him and her get together at the end, but it won't be for lack of feckin' trying.

MUCK:

I MANAGED: 20 pages, 6 diagrams.

SECRET DIARY OF A CALL GIRL
BELLE DE JOUR

PLOT: It's like *Fanny Hill* again, but it's got her from *Doctor Who* in it. Lighter weight, which might be handy.

MUCK:

I MANAGED: Back cover.

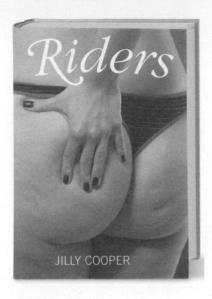

JILLY COOPER

FIFTY SHADES OF GREY E.L. JAMES

PLOT: This billionaire makes this poor woman go on a feckin' horrible diet, wallops the bejaysus out of her arse, and buys her loads of those plastic cable tidy things Mark did the back of the telly with. A proper man's gift, that. What's wrong with some feckin' flowers? She gets tied up and hit on the arse again. It's like one of them hostage books where your man's manacled to a radiator, but blue.

MUCK:

I MANAGED: All of.

FANNY HILL JOHN CLELAND

PLOT: I picked this up thinking it was a biography of the old 'Fastest Milkman in the West' fella, but it's even better than that. This girl in olden times (after cavemen but before *Downton Abbey*) becomes a brasser and has all sorts of shenanigans with men heaving and humping their startling big pant-pipes about like they're stealing a carpet. It is quite a big book though, so you need both hands to hold it, which sort of defeats the point.

MUCK:

I MANAGED: 8 pages.

RIDERS JILLY COOPER

PLOT: Posh English people ride each other and horses. No big surprise there. But the animal stuff's a bit harsh.

MUCK:

I MANAGED: 30 pages.

LADY CHATTERLEY'S LOVER
D.H. LAWRENCE

PLOT: I heard they banned this back in the day, which is a shame. It's got a proper *Upstairs Downstairs* thing going on, with most of the good stuff happening downstairs, plus some handy gardening tips.

MUCK:

I MANAGED: 20 pages.

• •

MY SECRET GARDEN
NANCY FRIDAY

PLOT: Feck knows, but if this book was a dog, it'd be after humping your leg. And your woman writing it would probably join in. Straight-up kinky, that's what it is, the stuff they get up to. I wouldn't say it had the strongest story, and I couldn't work out what happened to the twin uncles in the peephole rubber kilts, or the Nazi football team with the specially adapted submarine, for that matter, but I'll be honest, I wasn't paying attention.

MUCK:

I MANAGED: All of it. Twice.

• •

FORGIVE ME FATHER MASTURBATION FOR CATHOLICS

PLOT: There's more telling off in here than in that *Fifty Shades* one. Quite strict, if you like that sort of thing, but could do with a bit more romance and a bit less about the flames of hell. Hot, but not in a good way.

MUCK:

I MANAGED: 2 pages.

• •

I hope these bring you as much pleasure as they have me, and, judging by the fingernail gouges on her bedside table, Winnie. After all, we're flying solo most of the time these days, us two, and we still have our needs.

And as always, don't forget to wash your hands.

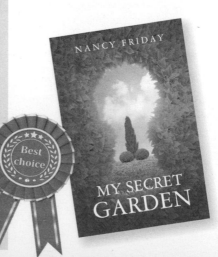

Eating

Aside from bringing her children into the world in the first place, a Mammy's biggest job is ensuring they get some good, honest food down their necks, so that they grow up fit and healthy.

And, of course, making certain her man gets a decent meal in him after a tough afternoon at the bookmakers.

Food is the foundation of a home. Not literally, or your walls would collapse. But like Napoleon's army, or Drambuie Mick leaving Foley's of a Friday, a family marches on its stomach.

Think of those big family meals – Christmas, Easter, weddings, wakes – all of you sat together, sharing and joking, confiding, confessing, reminiscing, pulling a cracker and putting on a colourful paper hat (or a black one if it's a wake) – and all accompanied by the warm, welcoming smells drifting from the family stove. Ah, they bring back memories like nothing else.

Like that first big family Sunday roast after Redser passed away, God bless him. I think of him now whenever I walk past a burning building. I was absolutely fucking hammered. Pissed as a tramp, I was. Two brigade officers had to drag me from the kitchen before the flames reached my pinny. Proper family cooking. That's what it's all about.

Have you seen what passes for cooking nowadays on the box? All the TV chefs? The boys are all feckin' effing and jeffing, or roasting a giant artificial sprout made from minced moosemeat with a welder's torch, and the girls are so busy licking their feckin' fingers I'm surprised they can grip a fork.

That's not proper cooking. I'd like to see how they'd manage in a real family kitchen, when everyone drops round unannounced and all you've got to work with is Rice Krispies and a catering size jar of gherkins. I tell you, cooking doesn't get any feckin' tougher than that.

One time, I sat in the kitchen and worked out how many meals I've cooked in my time as a Mammy, and I can't remember how many it was, but I tell you it took feckin' ages. We had to get fish and chips in. The kids were starving.

My lot have always been good eaters. Nice hearty appetites and clean plates. No complaints here. There was one time when Rory turned his nose up at my toad in the hole and insisted he was vegetarian. I thought it must be to impress a girl; I knew it wouldn't last. He's always been a sausage-lover, that boy.

But all this gabbing won't get the taters on.
Let's cook!

There's a lot of advice now about what to feed your child. And it's getting worse. I saw the pile of books Mark and Betty had, and the feckin' library Dermot and Maria hauled into the house. God knows what Rory and Dino'll be after reading when they have theirs.

I've watched the youngsters making kids' tea. It's like feckin' *Masterchef*. All sorts of exotic how's-your-father that I never saw on my plate 'til I was a feckin' grown-up: reductions, garnishes, vegetables. All to get smeared up the walls and dropped round the high chair.

And when you've worn yourself out preparing some Gordon Blue concoction for the chisellers, what about you? You'll be too knackered to do anything but ask himself to pick you up something battered from the chipper on the way home, and soon you'll be waddling down the High Street carting round an arse like a net full of feckin' footballs.

Although it may seem it sometimes, a family isn't just the kids. You have to give equal attention to your man. I hated the idea that just because I was looking after a gaggle of ankle-biters Redser wouldn't get a proper meal when he got home. My trick was to make sure that everyone ate the same. It saves time and fuss if you're not making special meals for everybody. And sure, Redser learned to love mashed banana and Muppet pasta shapes from a tin.

On special occasions, I'd pour them onto a plate.

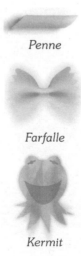

Penne

Farfalle

Kermit

5 A DAY

Your doctor will tell you that what you serve up to your family can affect more than their appetites. Not that I'd bother asking him something like that. At €50 a visit I want my feckin' tablets, not cookery advice. I can get that from the TV. In fact, there's almost feck all else on most of the time. Paul feckin' Hollywood. If he stuck his finger into my soggy bottom, I'd clout the daylights out of the cheeky bollix. But I do know it is important that your kids do get their five a day, or they're not having a balanced diet.

Here's how I give my lot their five a day.

....

Breakfast
2 sausages, fried

....

Lunch
1 sausage, fried and cut in half, in a sandwich

....

Dinner
2 sausages, fried

....

It's not that hard. Provided you have enough sausages.

FRUIT & VEG

Science these days says that, in addition to sausages, kids need vegetables, if only to keep their arses in good working order. The last thing you want to hear is the sound of them thrutching from the bathroom, going blue in the face like they're trying to squeeze a draught excluder through a keyhole.

But you know how it is – what with all the housework and bingo you never seem to have the right things in the house, and you realize they've had cheese on toast every day this week and their skin is starting to look like that paper that comes under the delivery pizza.

So, if you haven't quite managed to give your family any green stuff for a day or so, the following, I'm pretty certain, must count as fruit and vegetables, and are easy to slip into them as part of their regular diet.

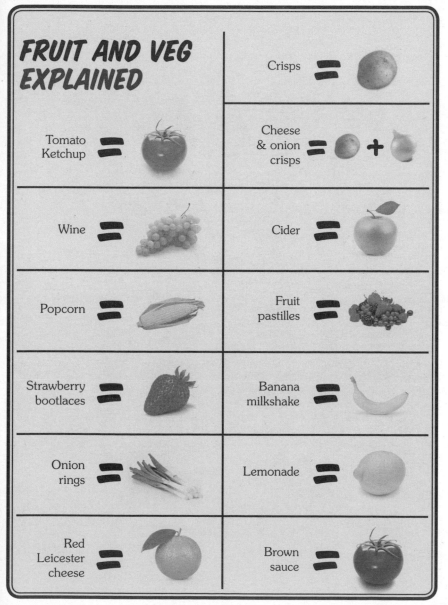

FRUIT AND VEG EXPLAINED

Crisps =

Tomato Ketchup =

Cheese & onion crisps = +

Wine =

Cider =

Popcorn =

Fruit pastilles =

Strawberry bootlaces =

Banana milkshake =

Onion rings =

Lemonade =

Red Leicester cheese =

Brown sauce =

COOKING
TIPS & TRICKS

FEATURING

Store-cupboard Standbys
Presentation
Menus
Mammy's Gravy
Eating Together
The Cookbook
Microwave Cooking
Recipes

REDUCED
FOR QUICK SALE
Now: 09c
CLEARANCE
10c

COOKING TIPS & TRICKS AGNES BROWN

That's
Nice
BOOK GR

AGNES BROWN PRESENTS

COOKING
TIPS & TRICKS

Here are some of the tricks I've picked up in all my years of pretending it's fish finger day again.

STORE-CUPBOARD STANDBYS

Just as Our Lord fed five thousand people using only five loaves, two fish and the power of God, one of the marks of a great Mammy is the ability to rustle up a meal at almost no notice.

And almost no notice is the precise amount of attention your family will pay you for doing it. The ungrateful feckers. I'd like to see them put together a last-minute gourmet dinner for eight using nothing but Weetabix, sardine paste and a cling-filmed catering tin of marrowfat peas. But I've done it. And had leftovers to spare. (Most of it, actually.)

You just have to always be prepared, and that means making sure you've got some basic store-cupboard standbys. To give you some idea, here's what's in my food cupboard right now.

- Tin of anchovy paste
- Bag of plain flour sealed with a peg
- Tin of mackerel fillets in brine (key snapped off)
- Bottle of lime flavour milkshake mix
- Tin of Doctor Who pasta shapes (Jon Pertwee)
- Jar of pickled walnuts
- Tin of chopped tomatoes (half price, dented)
- Tin of hot dogs (says use by 2004, but it's not bulging yet)

- Easy cook rice (in resealable bag)
- Easy cook rice (scattered over top shelf)
- Cornflour (3 x feckin' opened packets)
- Jars of pour-on sauce (bolognese, madras, salt 'n' vinegar)
- Lard x 2
- Steak pie in a tin (in case of air raid)
- Bottle of something furry in water (leaking)
- Dry pasta

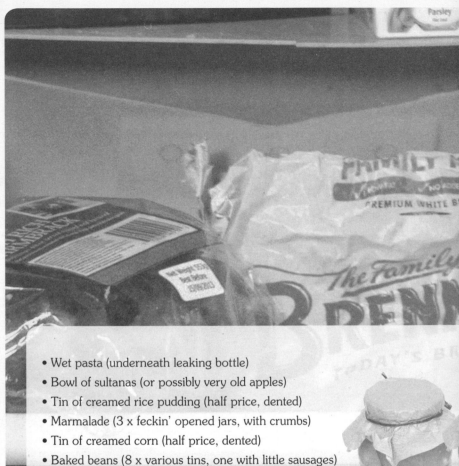

- Wet pasta (underneath leaking bottle)
- Bowl of sultanas (or possibly very old apples)
- Tin of creamed rice pudding (half price, dented)
- Marmalade (3 x feckin' opened jars, with crumbs)
- Tin of creamed corn (half price, dented)
- Baked beans (8 x various tins, one with little sausages)
- Pickle/chutney (4 x jars, all opened, some furry)
- Tin of cream of pilchard soup (half price, dented)
- Packet of mashed potato mix with a robot on the front
- Tin of Barry McGuigan pasta shapes (slightly rusty)
- Jar of piccalilli (use by 2005, Christmas leftover)
- Jar of piccalilli (use by 2006, Christmas leftover)
- Jar of piccalilli (use by 2009, Christmas leftover)

BEST BEFORE
DEC 2005

And with a selection like that, I know that my family are no more than half an hour away from a delicious dinner. Or, if it takes longer than 45 minutes to get here, a delicious dinner with free garlic bread and large Diet Coke.

MAMMY'S TIP

If you've created a dish from nothing, and the family love it, don't reveal what you've done. I remember making Mark and Betty a fish and leek pie using nothing more than chopped ham, sandwich spread and instant mash potato. 'This fish pie is really something else,' Betty said. And I knew how to take a compliment.

Presentation

No matter what you see Heston Bloomingtall do on the telly, presentation is more than dropping some grass on top and dribbling the ketchup round with your thumb over the bottle. It's about creating a special feeling with every meal you make. That's what Rory's Dino told me, and, as Rory never tires of telling me, he's a proper qualified chef. Which is why he works in a feckin' hairdresser's.

Rory always insists that Dino's food would get a star if only the Michelin man had had a chance to taste it. What would he know? I bet everything tastes of rubber to him. The bouncy great bollix.

MAMMY'S PRESENTATION TIPS

- Use a fork to smooth over thumbprints in mash.

- Wipe any splashes off dish edges with a towel (not the dog's one).

- Colour is important. Turn fish fingers so the burned parts are underneath.

- Leave space round food. That way there's more room for beans.

- Arrange longer, thinner items (asparagus, sausages) in a lattice.

- Make your rice look posh by putting it in a little cup and upending the cup onto the plate. Though this doesn't work with rice pudding. (And don't forget to remove the cup. Grandad still has nightmares about that china food he broke his falsers on.)

- Garnishes should be edible. Parsley or thyme, yes. Greengrocer's turf or Lego trees, no.

- Food looks better up in a pile than all spread out. Dino's tip, this, and all the chefs do it. I've seen him get spaghetti to stand on end.

- Different textures matter. So if you've done a really well-cooked bit of pork belly, and it's all crunchy, make sure you serve it with something soft. Like a napkin.

- Choose the right colour of crockery. A white dish for dark food, a darker one for pale food, and the dog's bowl for Grandad.

- Dusting. This is another thing Dino recommended to add a final flourish to a plate, but I find the taste of Pledge takes the zing out of a shepherd's pie.

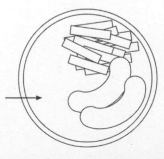

Figure 1
Space around food is important. That way there's more room for beans

Café de Mammy

Don't just dollop it up, describe it. You don't need fancy menus, just a serving hatch to shout through.

'What are we having, Mammy?' you hear.

You might want to shout 'Fritters' and get back to the hob, but be imaginative! Get their taste buds going with some of Dino's ten-Euro words. 'Pan-fried', 'seared', 'sun-dried' or 'on a bed of'. It'll distract them from the sound of the extractor fan on full and the thick smoke pouring through the serving hatch.

Actually, I can't bring myself to do that. It doesn't seem right. 'Pan-fried'? What else would I be feckin' frying it in? A bucket?

Still, it's all the rage now, using five words where one will do. Cathy took me to that new 'gastro pub' where Mulligan's

used to be. I've never seen a menu like it. I've read shorter Mills & Boons. And the ending was shite. I wouldn't be giving anything away if I said the coffee did it. I hope I haven't spoiled it for you.

'Gastro pub', I ask you! You'd think they'd cover that up, not advertize it. I've had gastro and it feckin' ruined Christmas. But if you're dishing up for guests, nothing impresses more than a bit of foreign when you describe the food. I can't deny it, 'bolognese' sounds better than 'mince with ketchup stirred in'.

This is proper useful if you've got someone stuck-up coming round. And I do mean you, Hilary Nicolson. Who the feck turns up to your home and doesn't even bring a bottle? Money can't buy you class. But it can buy you a fucking four-pack of Bulmers.

LITTLE EIFFEL TOWER

Fillets de poisson en croûte

fish fingers

Viande hachée d'une boîte avec
purée de petits pois

*Mince from a tin
and mushy peas*

Sac de frites avec un oeuf dur mariné

*Bag of chips
with a
Pickled Egg*

LITTLE LEANING
TOWER OF PISA

**Salsicce di Superquinn
e morsi alfabetici**

*Superquinn's
sausages and
alphabites*

**Triangoli di formaggio spalmata
sul pane tostato**

*cheese spread
triangles
on toast*

**Cose dalla parte posteriore del
frigorifero con stasera pollo**

*stuff from the back of the
fridge with 'Chicken Tonight'*

MAMMY'S GRAVY

There's nothing like the taste of Mammy's homemade gravy.
It's that flavour of home that they say you can't get anywhere else.
What's the secret? Ah! That'd be telling.

IT'S AN OXO CUBE. AND WATER.

I'd say this was medium rare but it's all too common.

They call me the Domestos Goddess.

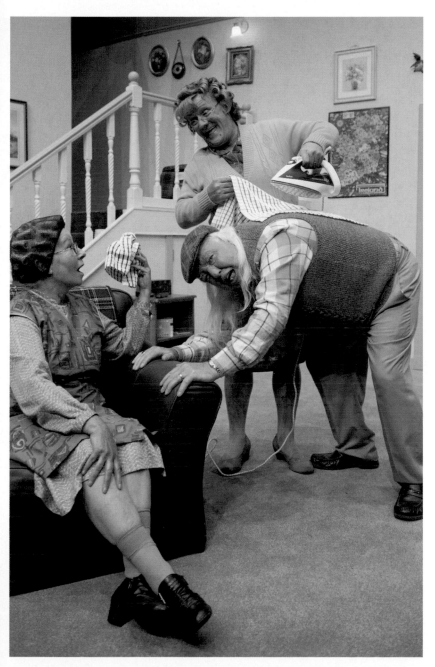

There's no need to iron tea towels but this is too much fun.

Are people going to know this is Dial-a-Dick if we can only see his arse?

This is my favourite page
in the whole book
Hope I haven't spoiled it for you.

A balanced diet includes food and drink.

Can't help thinking of my wedding night! When we had sausages.

YOU WILL NEED: an Oxo cube, some water.

METHOD: boil the water briskly for five minutes. Stir in the Oxo cube.

To thicken the gravy, add cornflour a minute or two before serving dinner, when it's refusing to get any thicker than rusty rainwater and you're swearing like a feckin' sailor, and strain out the white lumps with the cabbage sieve.

Store any leftover gravy in the fridge in a tea cup until you knock it over.

—

MAMMY'S TIP
Remove the foil before stirring in the Oxo cube, so it dissolves faster.

EATING TOGETHER

If there's one thing I know it's that it's important for a family to eat together. And if there's one other thing I know, it's the names of the Magnificent Seven. There's a €30 prize at Foley's pub quiz and we've all got our strengths. They say that children who eat at a table with the whole family are 40% less likely to have problems with diet or alcohol abuse, 35% more likely to have a stable marriage and 12% more likely to become statisticians. It's a good solid career, that, so I don't throw that figure out there lightly.

There's a terrible habit that's developed in the younger generation of taking your tea on your lap in front of the television. But how's a child meant to learn how to have a proper conversation, or good manners, stuck in front of the box?

Children who eat at the table

40% less likely to have problems with diet or alcohol abuse

35% more likely to have a stable marriage

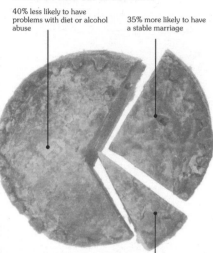

12% more likely to become statisticians.

Unless there's a programme about good manners or maybe a chat show on. And then, they'd be looking at their dinner all the time and missing the good bits. As it is, they're more likely to end up watching some feckin' shite where a load of people burst into tears with stress trying to make more and more complicated food and arrange it on a huge plate in a tiny pile with a twig on top. That kind of nonsense can put a kid off their spaghetti hoops.

The best way is the old way. Whether it's you and one child who needs their Mammy, or every man jack of them huddled round the kitchen table, talking, swapping stories, passing the pepper, eating together is the family at its best. Whether they want it or not.

Persuading a family member to stay and eat against their will

Sometimes a family member will drop in and not want to stay for food. Nobody wants to handcuff them to the radiator – that only works once – but it's important they stay and eat.

Follow this simple flowchart next time the door flaps open, and you'll never eat alone.

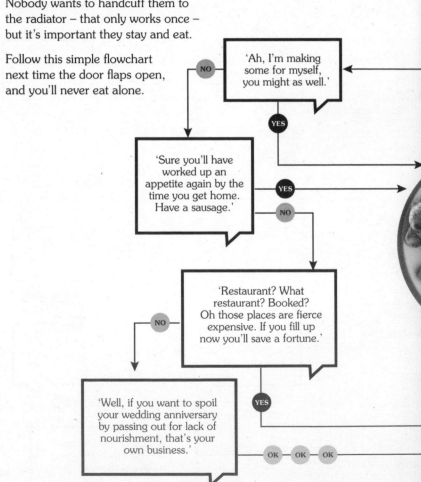

NO

'Ah, I'm making some for myself, you might as well.'

YES

'Sure you'll have worked up an appetite again by the time you get home. Have a sausage.'

YES

NO

'Restaurant? What restaurant? Booked? Oh those places are fierce expensive. If you fill up now you'll save a fortune.'

NO

YES

'Well, if you want to spoil your wedding anniversary by passing out for lack of nourishment, that's your own business.'

OK — OK — OK

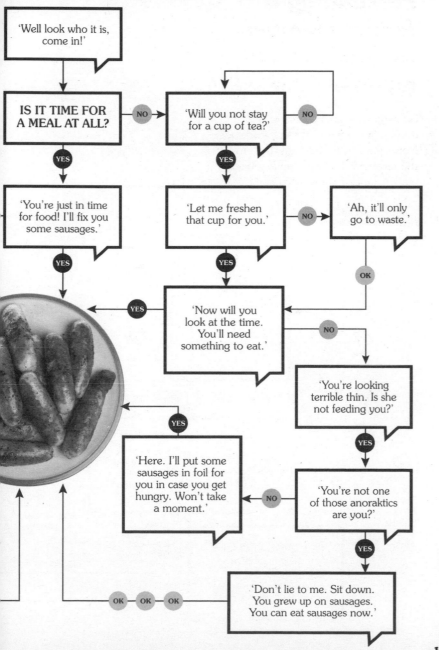

'Well look who it is, come in!'

IS IT TIME FOR A MEAL AT ALL?

NO → 'Will you not stay for a cup of tea?' NO

YES

'You're just in time for food! I'll fix you some sausages.'

YES

'Let me freshen that cup for you.' NO → 'Ah, it'll only go to waste.'

YES

OK

'Now will you look at the time. You'll need something to eat.'

YES →

NO

'You're looking terrible thin. Is she not feeding you?'

YES

'Here. I'll put some sausages in foil for you in case you get hungry. Won't take a moment.'

YES →

NO ← 'You're not one of those anoraktics are you?'

YES

OK OK OK

'Don't lie to me. Sit down. You grew up on sausages. You can eat sausages now.'

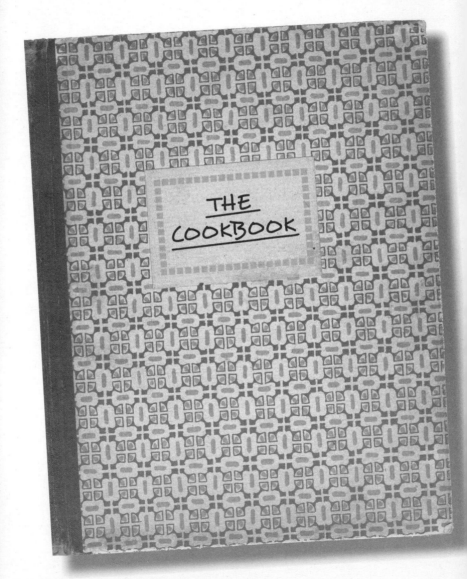

THE
COOKBOOK

Every Mammy has some standby dishes
that will always bring the family to the table.
Often they're the things your Mammy taught
you. It's one of my fondest memories: my
own Mammy taking me to the kitchen and
showing me the basics, even though I was
only three, fumbling and making a terrible
mess, barely able to reach the hob. She'd
been drinking for hours. I won't forget my
first time in charge of a chip pan.

But these were skills without which she said I could never be
a wife and mother myself. And, God love her, she was right.

You need three basic dishes, that was what my Mammy told
me. They're not hard, but they'll never let you down. And,
even though she's not had cause to use them yet, I passed
those old family favourites on to Cathy, for when her time
comes. It might seem old-fashioned, but I don't think any
daughter should leave the family nest without knowing how
to make the basics.

1. Toast
2. Sausages
3. Whatever the other one was

Those are the solid foundations of a family menu.
But a family can't live on toast and sausages and
whatever the other one was forever. They need variety.
This is where your cookbook comes in.

IMPORTANT:

Make sure your handwriting's clear. Voice of experience, here: there's a world of difference between a pinch of salt and a pint!

As a special treat, I've had the lads at the publishers type up a few favourite scraps from my very own kitchen bible!

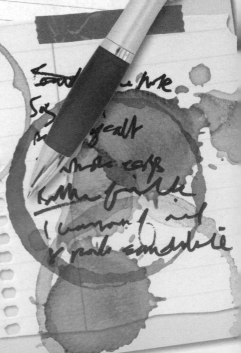

TOAD IN THE HOLE

- 5oz of flob
- pinch of sand
- 3 whore eggs
- Boom! of milk
- 1 tampon of oil
- 8 pork sandwiches

N.B.
PLEASE PROOF-
READ THIS!
DANIEL

****

Brown sandwiches in oil. Add a pinch of sand. Whisk flob, eggs, milk until better, pour on sandwiches, 35 min at 2000 C. Serves A.

8 pork sandwiches

TORNADO AND CARPET SOUP

- 4 large chapped carpets
- 1 union
- 1 tit chapped tornadoes
- 1 gaelic glove
- 1 tampon gran corridor
- ½ tampon gran grainger
- ½ tampon gran cinema
- ½ tampon patrick
- ½ tampon gran cumming
- ½ tampon gran lunatic
- 2 waters
- 2 vegetable sock pubes
- 2 deserts poohcaster Shergar
- 1 deserts pooh tornado puree
- pinch of sand
- pinch of gran Blue Peter
- 6 fl oz dong cream

A gaelic glove

****

Bring ingredients to boil on hop and summer for 45 mins.
Bland thoroughly before serving. Serves 6.

IRISH STEW

- 2 tampons of oil
- 1lb lamb c**t (let's cut into chunks)
- 2lb King Egg word-potatoes (quartered)
- 4oz chapped union
- 3oz sluiced leaks
- 2 large chapped carpets
- 1½ pints beer stock
- 3oz sliced cobbage
- pinch of sand
- pinch of gran Blue Peter

Tampons of oil x2

****

Brown pieces of lamb c**t, lets in oil. Place incasserole with vag.
Addstock, cover, cook 1 hour. Add cobbage and cook 1 more hour.
Season with sand and Peter. Serves G.

*And it's those smells, those flavours, that mean no matter how far
your birds fly from Mammy's, they'll always come home.*

MICROWAVE COOKING

Sometimes time is more important than taste, and for that there's the microwave oven. You can cook anything in the microwave, as long as you don't mind it not being very nice. Don't ask me how a microwave works, but it must be something to do with coating food in hot rubber, because that's what it feckin' does to fish fingers. I've seen more appetizing things come out the back of the dog.

I don't generally hold with microwaving myself. The old ways are the best when it comes to cooking. A good, slow-cooked Irish stew. A full roast dinner with all the trimmings. Lemon curd on a digestive biscuit. You can't do them in a microwave properly. You need a big old-fashioned oven to do them justice (except the lemon curd and

now I wish I'd thought of a better example there).

The lads who make the microwaves want you to do everything in the feckers, though. There's a picture of a feckin' roast chicken on the dial of mine. A roast chicken! I think it's just for decoration. I mean, there's an apple on the back of Maria's phone, but you're not meant to make crumble with the fecker. You show me someone who microwaves their Sunday roast, and I'll show you someone who's quietly lost the feckin' will to live.

That's not to say they're entirely useless. Stuff-in-a-cup – a recipe invented by Dermot and refined by yours truly – has revolutionized teatime and halved the washing up.

STUFF-IN-A-CUP

YOU WILL NEED

- stuff
- a cup

METHOD

Pour the stuff into the cup.
Put the cup in the microwave for
90 seconds at full whack. Remove
and eat, with a tea towel over your
hands to avoid third degree burns.

*Can feed a family of six
with five minutes' notice.*

BASIC STUFF-IN-A-CUP

Beans, spaghetti shapes, tinned plum tomatoes, mash, soup

ADVANCED STUFF-IN-A-CUP

Leftover casserole, pilchards, cheese on toast, whole lobster (for guests)

Oh, and re-heating cups of tea. That's what microwaves are good for. You'll be doing that a lot. When the chisellers were small, Jaysus, but I never finished a whole cup of tea. You stagger round after they're tucked up in bed, spotting cold cups left everywhere, like little 'MAMMY WAS HERE' markers. But it's simplicity itself to pop a half-finished cup of tea into the microwave, give it a minute on full power, and then forget it's in the microwave until you find it there again next morning, stone cold.

I do use the microwave to defrost, though. It's handy to be able to grab a tupperware of unidentified leftovers out of the freezer, zap it in the microwave for ten minutes and find out that it's not something you fancy eating. (How come EVERYTHING you freeze ends up looking like the liquidized contents of a hoover bag? Science should be working this out instead of pissing around with Hardon Colliders.) You can then scoop the stuff easily into the bin without needing to chip it out with a knife.

A microwave oven is also a first class way to find out which of your cups and bowls breaks in a microwave oven. If there's nothing on the telly, I put a gilt-edged souvenir plate in there, settle down in front of the oven with a cold cup of tea and pretend it's live coverage of the New Year's fireworks. Sometimes it even sounds like it.

DINO'S
RECIPES

by Dino Doyle
including foreword by Agnes Brown

FOREWORD

Dino says he's a chef. What a chef's doing
working in a bucking hairdresser's is beyond me.
Blue-rinsing the vegetables?
Putting some poor cow's hair in barbecue tongs?
Pouring a nice cold glass of shampoo?

Whatever he's up to, it's got sweet Fanny
Cradock to do with food, I'll tell you.

Anyway, he said wouldn't it be grand if he put a
couple of his recipes in Mammy's book, and I
said no, and he said ah go on, and Rory chipped
in with some emotional bucking blackmail about
how it'd be good for his career and – well, the
long and short of it is that I needed a few pages
off (I haven't had a cup of tea since p.27) so I'm
letting him loose.

Mind you, if he tries any of his fancy-pants New-
Bell Cuisine, I'll be changing it. You see if I feckin'
don't. I'm not having my book full of drizzles. It's
bad enough having Grandad drizzling over his
food, without a qualified cook joining in.

Most of these modern chefs are just changing
words for the sake of it, I tell you. I heard one the
other day on the TV saying he was making a
'redcurrant joo'. I had to shout at the telly, I
couldn't help my feckin' self: 'It's pronounced
GOO.' Eejits.

Agnes Brown

~~LAMB'S~~ LIVER WITH ~~STICKY~~ ONIONS AND ~~CRISPY~~ BACON

*Keep it feckin' simple Dino!
No one wants to know where their
food comes from*

Oh my god he's on terrorists now.

Liver can melt in the mouth if it's seared quickly. That velvety pink flesh should be rich and yielding, yet resolutely al dente. The combination of rich liver, tart sticky onions reduced in red wine vinegar, and crispy strips of dry-cured bacon is absolutely heavenly. *You speak for yourself. Livers always felt like boiled eyes to me unless it's done properly.*

INGREDIENTS

350g lamb's liver
*stop talking about the poor
little lambs, will you?*

3 medium-sized onions

50g butter
like anybody weighs butter!

3 tablespoons red wine vinegar *All
red wine tastes like bucking vinegar to me. I
think it's cause him at the Mace keeps it in
the window.*

6 rashers dry-cured bacon (back)
back of what? The fridge?

a little oil
I'm telling you it's lard you want

*Never mind this shite. Fry the liver and
bacon and stick them on a plate. How
hard can it be? Anything else is a feckin'
distraction. Right. That's quite enough
of that.*

SERVES 2

*There's one born
every minute*

Peel the onions, and cut them into six segments. *Segments? What are they?
Terry's chocolate onions?*

Soften them slowly over a low heat in the oil, then, when they're sweet and sticky and are starting to catch, add the red wine vinegar and bring up the heat. *get to the point*

catch what?

Scoop the onions from the pan, put them aside and keep them warm. Then wipe the pan with a kitchen towel. *Over my dead body. That pan's got years of flavour in it. You know nothing.*

Slice the liver thinly. Melt the butter in the pan over a high heat and, when it's sizzling, add the liver. When the liver has browned, turn it over and cook for another minute. *You need a feckin' stopwatch for this.*

Set the liver aside to warm plates. Then fry off the finely diced bacon until it is crisp and crunchy. Add the onion to the pan. Stir everything together in the juices, and serve immediately with crushed potatoes.

Us humans call it mash.

CLASSIC BANGERS AND MASH
WITH A TWIST

Keep your smut out of my book

If you've ever had tradesmen in your home, you'll know that nothing satisfies a working man like a hot sausage. There's simply nothing as heartwarming and wholesome as coarsely chopped pork and herbs, slowly fried to a sticky conclusion to bring out all those glorious flavours, sat proudly on a bed of silkily buttered mash. *Still sounds rude to me...*

INGREDIENTS

6 ~~good quality pork and leek~~ sausages
450g floury potatoes (King Edwards)
A good knob of butter
50ml cream
Don't think I don't know what you're up to
Salt and pepper *They're on the table*
~~A little oil~~ *A lot of lard*

SERVES ~~2~~

fry
~~Arrange~~ the sausages in a ~~cast iron~~ frying pan ~~over a low heat. Add a little oil to the pan – just enough to stop them sticking. Leave the sausages to cook slowly, turning them once or twice to keep the browning on the skins nice and even. Half an hour on a low heat will result in a lovely sticky sausage.~~

~~Meanwhile,~~ peel and chop the potatoes ~~into medium-sized chunks~~ and boil them in salted water. ~~Don't add the salt until the water is on the boil; this could tarnish the pan.~~ →*BOLLIX.*
When the potatoes are tender, drain them, return to the pan and stir in the butter and cream.

Scoop the mash onto the plates, and lay the sausages across the top. *You don't say? And wasn't I going to serve them up in a shoe box*

peas
Serve with ~~a thick, rich onion gravy, made with a hearty glass of red wine. Season with salt and pepper~~ and mash the potatoes ~~to a firm, silky consistency~~ with a ~~potato ricer or potato masher.~~ *feckin' fork*

Beauty

HOW NOT TO
LET YOURSELF GO

You get to a certain age and there's a terrible temptation to let yourself go. For Winnie that certain age was 23.

I say to Winnie, you've got to look after yourself. No other fecker's going to. You don't want your Jacko to get a wandering eye. Though it'd make the full set with his cauliflower ear and spastic colon.

In my day, we didn't have all these liposuctions and Bollox injections. We had to make the best of what the Good Lord gave us. That, and a fist of Kleenex down each cup for luck. By the time a lad found out you were packing hankies, it was too late. *(Fair's fair, my first date with Redser, he stuffed a football sock down his pants. I told him, you feckin' idiot, you're supposed to put it down the front.)*

MAKE THE BEST OF WHAT
THE GOOD LORD GAVE US

Fistful of Kleenex down your feckin' bra

Dressing well

You can keep your Vivian Westworlds and your Donna Nutella Versace. Dressing well is all about bras.

Bras. Yes. And, no, I will not feckin' modify my language.

You've got to wear the right bra. No matter if you're flat-chested, well stacked or a man in a dress, full support is essential for an attractive womanly figure.

I remember getting my Cathy fitted for her first training bra. Honest to God, it was more of a ritual than a practical necessity. Back then she was flatter than Pavarotti's sofa cushions. But as she turned to me that day in the changing room, I had a tear in my eye. I knew my little girl was a woman. And, as a bonus, with the bra on, I could finally tell which way round she was facing.

I'd brought up so many boys by then, I tell you, it was a magical moment. I liked the ritual so much, I took Dermot to get fitted for a bra of his own when he hit twelve. He didn't thank me. Oh, the others teased him. For a start, he took a cup size up from Cathy.

They say if you can get a pencil under each boob, you need a bra. If you can't find the pencil afterwards, you need underwiring.

Besides, an underwired bra is the perfect way to prepare a girl for motherhood.

Comfort, security, and the regular stabbing pain around the heart.

It's vital to ensure you're wearing the right size. You can get measured in a shop, but then you're a sitting duck for a terrible hard sell. *You'll come away with three or four bras, and you with only the two tits.*

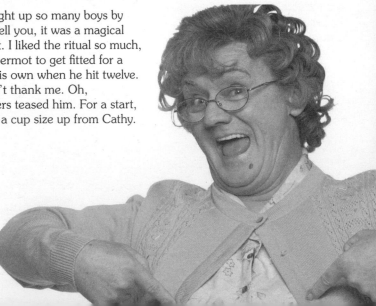

It's a simple matter to measure yourself at home.

Take a measurement yourself under the bust with a tape measure.
A dressmaker's one will do. Not one of those steel ones from Mark's
toolbox that comes back at a clip. Fuck me. You only make that
mistake once. Then use this handy chart to estimate the correct cup
size, using things you can easily find around the kitchen.

Coaster	AA
Ashtray	A
Tea cup	B
Cocoa mug	C
Sugar bowl	D
Cereal bowl	E
Mixing bowl	F
Washing up bowl	G
Bin	G+*

*Anything bigger than that and
you'd better call the circus.

Mammy's Tip
The same home-measuring trick works
with children's shoes. When a child's
feet are too big to fit the box the
shoes came in, you need to buy
new ones.

UNWANTED HAIR

Most women only want hair on one place: their husband's head.

But so many of us, God help us, are denied even that. Redser always boasted he had the same full thick hair as Cary Grant. Only problem was it was mainly on his arse. I've seen what happens to men past middle age: all the hair moves off the head and comes bristling out everywhere else – ears, nose, eyebrows – till the poor bastard looks like a boiled sweet picked off a barber's floor.

Face it. With him like an exploded scarecrow, and you patting thick foundation over the beginnings of a Stalin moustache, someone has to take things in hand, or every time you and your man step outside the front door, people are going to mistake you for a folk festival or one of those gorilla invasions you see at the pictures.

But science has the answer! If you watch the better TV channels (the ones in the 600s with a nice lad hawking all sorts from a podium) you can pick up a wide range of hair removal whatnots, many of which aren't available in the shops for some reason.

Some people don't like to shop off the TV. Winnie, for example, doesn't like to give her details over the phone in case gangsters steal her identity and use it to pull off crimes. Jaysus only knows what they'd do with it. Holding up a bank with Winnie McGoogan masks? That's the unacceptable face of feckin' lawbreaking right there. Any master criminal steals Winnie's identity, the police'll know where to find them sure enough. Down the feckin' bingo.

Anyway, if you, like Winnie, are still living in the feckin' Dark Ages, there are plenty of good hair-removal products on the high street. You just have to shop around.

I got this cracking electric hair trimmer for Grandad down the market one time. Lovely box with a picture of that Nikita Khrushchev on it. Must have been cheap because of a printing error: all the Rs were back to front. I could only get the plug in the socket by snapping off one of the pointy bits and having at it with a hammer. But it certainly took the hair out of his ears. And most of the skin off my feckin' arms.

To be honest, we all ended up living in the Dark Ages that day until our Mark came round and got the electric working again.

Or you can always use scissors. A small set of needlework scissors are best, or if you're dealing with the tougher hair of the more elderly gentleman, a pair of gardening gloves, some secateurs and a bucking good run-up.

Do wait till they're asleep, though, or they might think you're coming at them for the life insurance.

Agnes's
TOP TELESHOPPING
Hair Removal
PRODUCTS

CHANNEL 614

Gallagher eyebrow wax

€9.99

Agonizing. Pulls harder than Winnie's Sharon down Foley's the week before Valentines.

STAR CHOICE!

CHANNEL 677

Qualpunch earmower

€29.99

It's a lot less bovver with a hover.

CHANNEL 623

Brevlon nasal defoliant

€14.99

Based on that fierce stuff they dropped out of helicopters in Vietnam. Brings up pans a treat.

brevlon
nasal defoliant

Fuzgo loganberry smoothing cream

€15.00

Delicious. Ate the whole jar before I could try it on Grandad's ears, but it works! My tongue's as hairless as a baby's balls.

Drax industries nasal laser

€149.99

Hair never grows back, but the beam did cut Grandad's armchair in half.

STAR CHOICE!

Zylax depilatory paste

€74.99

Took all the hair off in one go, also stripped the dog bare as a worm, and unblocked the straggly build up in the bath overflow.

BIKINI WAXING

A lady of a certain age can get powerful hairy below, and even the most 'bohemian' woman should make some attempt to be beach-ready. I've seen magazines down the dentist you wouldn't feckin' believe, and there is one lesson stands out loud and clear: you never know when the paraparaparazzi might come snapping around your undercarriage like rats at an upturned butcher's bin, and I mean that warning as a kindness.

*Here's how to tidy your ladybasement.**

1.
PURCHASE YOUR MATERIALS

You will need some good waxing strips, a trimming razor, and half a bottle of Scotch with a quick-release cap. Trust me. You want to be able to whip into that thing faster than feckin' Zorro.

2.
MAKE A PLAN

What shape do you want? Brazilian? Love heart? Landing strip? No Entry sign? I'm not kidding. Some women I know, it'd be a feckin' mercy. Anyway, try designing the shape you want first on paper. For added realism, you could use iron filings. Or cut a stencil out of a scourer.

3.
TAKE A SHOWER

A warm shower will soften the hairs. Good luck with getting a shower if your house is anything like mine, with people popping in and out all hours of the day and night using your facilities like it's a feckin' TV studio. A quick mop over the required area with a dishcloth is about all you're going to get. If you're worried about using a dishcloth and getting hairs on your washing-up, use a moistened blanket from the dog basket. Hygiene is everything.

> **Mammy's Tip**
> You can always gather the trimmings and stuff a cushion. Or, in Grandad's case, a three-piece suite.

4.
FIND SOMEWHERE QUIET

This is an intimate, private moment. Again, if your home's like mine, you might want to hide in the cupboard under the stairs or pop into the garage. Make sure there's somewhere to throw away the used strips. You could just do it outside by the bins. That's probably more private than my bucking front room.

5.
TEST WAX TEMPERATURE

Dab a little wax on your wrist to make sure it's a comfortable temperature before applying. That's important. It's not like you're about to do anything feckin' uncomfortable now, is it?

6.
ADOPT THE CORRECT POSITION

To remove hair from the front of your intimate area, sit with feet on the floor, knees bent, legs apart. To get at the more difficult-to-reach hairs, simply train for twelve years with the feckin' Romanian Olympic gymnastics team until you can get your ankles behind your feckin' ears. Or ask Mary Flanagan how she managed to service that pipe band in the back of an Austin Maxi out the back of Quinnsworth. She'll have some feckin' tips, I'll wager.

7.
APPLY AND REMOVE WAX

Yeah. That sounds pretty feckin' straightforward, doesn't it? 'All in one smooth movement.' No trouble at all. Feckin' idiots. 'Step seven. Bite your own leg off.' No. You feckin' do it. They can put a man on the feckin' moon to play golf, but they can't come up with a better way of thinning your draught excluder than boiling a candle on to your foof and ripping the shite out of it. What did I do to deserve this? It's the sort of thing a captain would have done to punish mutineers.

8.
SCOTCH

Told you you'd want it.

9.
FECK IT

Give up. Go and buy some bigger feckin' knickers. Or grow it long and pretend it's a pair of thick tights. Winter's coming on. You'll feel the benefit.

*This is based on the instructions from a box of FUZGO LADYWAX (Channel 672, €13.99), but I got wax and hair all over some of the descriptions, so I'm expanding from experience. What the feck do they know anyway? All those leaflets are written by men. You can tell. It's why they look like instructions for putting up a shelf. If I did them, there'd be pictures of what your feckin' face looked like while you tried to rip your short and curlies out with feckin' Super Glue and Sellotape. Just as a warning. I mean, Jaysus, I've had easier childbirths.

Dieting

I had quite the figure in my day.
I'd get so many whistles walking
down the street I thought I was being
stalked by Roger feckin' Whittaker.

But it gets harder to maintain that hourglass figure. Soon you're struggling to achieve 'pint glass', and before you know it, you'd settle for 'goldfish bowl'.

It's wrong to be obsessed with your own appearance – vanity is a sin just the same as sloth or coveting thy neighbour's tiebacks – but it's nice to know that someone passing you in the street would recognize you as a woman, rather than a group of refugees huddling under a cardigan.

I always say, don't change your appearance for a man. Do it for yourself. Unless you're a man, in which case, fair enough.

So to avoid that inevitable day when you need to be freed from the revolving doors at Penney's with the jaws-of-life, you decide to take yourself in hand, before it gets so nobody else will.

It's time to diet.

SIZE ZERO

It seems like everyone's on a
feckin' diet these days. I suppose
it's the photos in the magazines.
Skinny fucking things, all nine-
inch waists and legs like spaghetti
with a knot in it, prannying about
on the beach in less fabric than
I use to blow my feckin' nose.
It warps your expectations. Most
of us aren't that shape. I don't
think I've ever seen anyone that
shape. Charles Hawtrey, maybe?

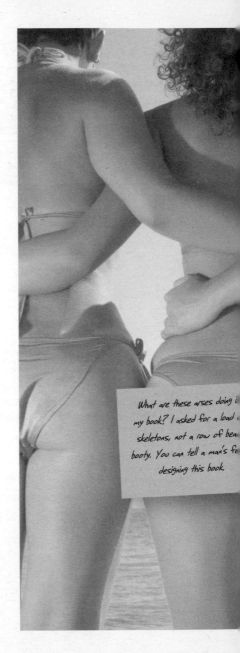

What are these arses doing i
my book? I asked for a load
skeletons, not a row of bea
booty. You can tell a man's fe
designing this book

Look at the state of these. And that's supposed to be attractive now, is it? *I've seen more meat on a feckin' biro.* Last time I saw something like the poor wretch on the left, it dropped on me in a ghost train.

I'm not saying there's anything wrong with being thin, if you're a thin sort of person. I knew a girl at school, Theresa Sweeney, who ate like a Roman emperor and never put on a smidge of weight. She could hide behind wallpaper. Six foot tall, and huge great feet she had. With the light behind her, you'd mistake her for a golf club.

People come in all shapes and sizes, but you wouldn't know it looking at the magazines. Why can't just one of these girls be a normal feckin' size? I suppose she'd be worried the others would eat her. And they'd still be hungry after that. Doesn't look like any one of them's seen a decent feckin' sausage in ages. Though, to be honest, can you be surprised? No real man's going for a woman who looks like that. He'd graze his knuckles on their ribs.

It's not just women who feel the pressure. Dermot promised Maria he'd lose weight before the wedding by following this fancy diet she'd found. I told him she should love him no matter what he weighed. It's what's inside that counts. Unfortunately, what was inside was mainly chips.

Anyway, he followed the diet and it made no feckin' difference at all. You can't force an elephant to change its spots, I suppose. But at least he tried.

If you want to lose a few pounds, here's how to do it.

MAMMY'S DIET PLAN

My Cathy wrote this diet plan out for me, and it worked, with the few adjustments I've made here. I think she copied it from one of her books. I'm guessing she couldn't lend me the book because one night she'd gone mental with hunger, ripped all the pictures out of it and boiled them down to make soup.

Some people have trouble sticking to diets, but it's easy if you follow some simple rules.

1.

Take it one meal at a time.

2.

Try not to eat between meals, but if you need to have some raisins or a piece of fruit to keep your energy up, don't feel ashamed.

3.

Make it achievable. If you can't get hold of all the ingredients, feel free to replace them with something you do have, and don't get discouraged.

4.

Hide the biscuits!

Monday

BREAKFAST

Fresh fruit and natural yoghurt

LUNCH

Fresh tuna and egg salad

DINNER

Grilled chicken kebabs with
yoghurt and fresh salad

Tuesday

BREAKFAST

Organic porridge with
skimmed milk

LUNCH

Carrot sticks and low fat
dip

2p.m. - handful of Sugar Puffs to stave off hunger.

4.15 p.m. - handful of dry pasta to stop blacking out.

DINNER

Small grilled salmon steak
with 40g boiled rice

10.30 p.m.

80g dog biscuits.

Feckin' hell, I'm starving.

Wednesday

BREAKFAST

One ~~boiled~~ egg sandwich
  fried

LUNCH

~~Broccoli and beetroot salad with
green beans~~

Baked beans and sausages

DINNER

Red ~~mullet~~ with brown ~~rice~~
  sauce   sauce and sausages

Thursday

BREAKFAST

~~Yoghurt and banana~~
~~smoothie with almonds~~

          sausages

LUNCH

Cream of
~~Grilled~~ chicken *soup* breast and
all the green ~~salad~~
        ones from the Quality Street

DINNER

Baked potato and ~~small~~ tin
of ~~tuna~~

corned beef

    Filling up nicely now.

Friday

BREAKFAST

~~Halved grapefruit~~ th small
bag of ~~raisins and~~ ~~lnut~~
~~halves~~ *Wotsits*

LUNCH

~~Carrot and coriander soup with~~
~~wholemeal~~ roll
Swiss

DINNER

~~Mackerel bake with couscous and~~
~~red~~ pepper *oni and five cheese pizza*

Saturday

BREAKFAST
Cottage ~~cheese~~ *pie* and
rice ~~cracker~~
pudding

LUNCH
Scotch Egg ~~white omelette~~ with
~~green~~ salad *cream*

DINNER
~~Steamed~~ cod, *chips* ~~steak~~ and
~~mushrooms~~
↳ *y peas*

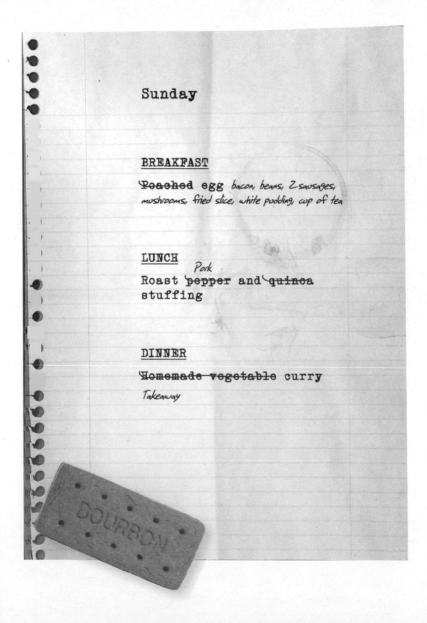

Sunday

BREKFAST

~~Poached~~ egg *bacon, beans, 2 sausages, mushrooms, fried slice, white pudding, cup of tea*

LUNCH

Pork

Roast ~~pepper~~ and ~~quinoa~~
stuffing

DINNER

~~Homemade vegetable~~ curry

Takeaway

You might think it'd be a job to stick to, but once I was up and going, I found reserves of willpower that I didn't even know I had. Would you believe that at the end of the week, I still had a full packet of digestives, hidden in the battery drawer, untouched?

Plus I had so much cheese and bread left over that I was able to reward myself with four days of nothing but cheese on toast three times a day. And if anyone says that's not a balanced diet, there's something wrong with their scales. *(There's definitely something wrong with mine. That 0 looks like a 6.)*

I find it a source of great pride that, all these years after my wedding, I can still fit into the dress my mother wore that day.

Monday

Tuesday

Wednesday

Thursday

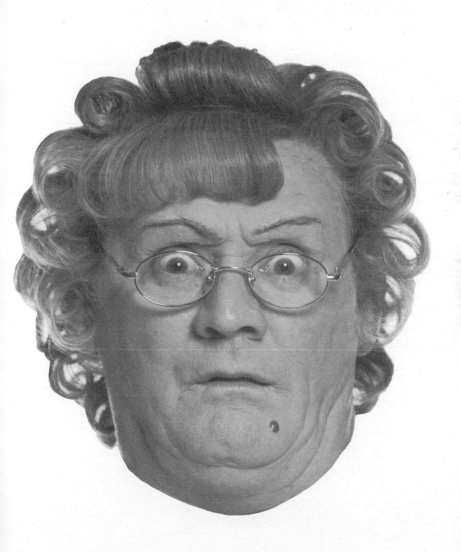

See what you could look like after following my diet.

Injuries ✚ Accidents

Doesn't matter how well you keep your home, accidents will happen. Especially with the chisellers. You could cover your house in bubble wrap and a toddler would find the one bit you'd left exposed and take his eye out on it. They're like feckin' kamikaze pilots, injuring themselves for the Emperor.

Maria and Dermot's place looks like a cross between a soft play area and a nuclear feckin' power station. They've got baby monitors, room thermometers, stair gates, a fire guard *(even though they haven't got a bucking fire)*, plastic corner cushions on their tables, things to stick in their plug sockets, things that stop the doors from closing, cupboard locks to stop doors from opening, pipe covers, hinge covers, tap covers – it's a wonder they had any time at all with the boys, with all the hours they must have spent installing it all. I wouldn't have been surprised if one of the kids had stabbed the other one with a rattle while their parents were off childproofing the place.

I had one safety precaution against my lot getting into scrapes: these two eyes. And they came ready-installed.

You often hear people say, *'You can't be too careful'*. Well, here's a little secret I'd like to share with you: Yes you fucking can. If you're disinfecting your windows, you've gone too far. Especially if you're doing them from the outside.

But every Mammy needs a bathroom cabinet with a few bits and pieces in it, just in case.

THE BATHROOM CABINET

First Aid Kit

Don't bother buying one of these from the shops, with all their funny little things in sealed envelopes. You can make one out of bits you've already got in the house, no problem.

+ Plasters
  (Sellotape)

+ Eye pads
  (cut up bits of old terry nappies)

+ Safety pins *(no idea why, but they're always in these boxes, so at least I know where the safety pins are)*

+ Something like a bandage
  (old tights)

+ Tracheotomy tube *(old biro)*

+ Pair of Marigolds

Medicines

You'll always need a good collection of medicines. Don't forget to check the dates on them. If they haven't got dates on them, they date from before they put dates on them, so it's time to throw them away.

• Cough medicines don't work. *None of them. So get a nice cheap bottle of linctus. At least that doesn't claim to have magical powers. At the price you pay for some cough medicines, you'd think that the childproof cap was to keep a feckin' genie inside.*

• Painkillers are right handy. *Keep a couple of bottles. I have cider and brandy, but there are some less tasty ones around, like aspirin (which you really need a mixer for) and parachutamol, which is more of an after-dinner painkiller. Sickly stuff.*

• Stuff for stings. *Little sprays and roll-ons. You can get free samples of deodorant from the chemist. Mind you, they do sting a bit when you put them on a wound. But sometimes you have to fight fire with fire.*

• Antihistameanies. *Didn't have these in my day. I think they're supposed to stop you sneezing or something. Maria always has some in her handbag. And you never hear her handbag sneeze, so they must work.*

• Smelling salts. *Good, old-fashioned medicine. I've still got the bottle my Mammy's Mammy handed down. And they still smell as bucking vile as ever. I don't know anyone who's ever got through a bottle of these, though I do keep mine out of reach of Grandad, just in case.*

Injuries

There's all sorts of scrapes and misfortunes that you can come a cropper of around the house: burns, cuts, falls, electric shocks, putting your foot through the ceiling when you're up in the loft. But the most common household injury, by an uphill mile, is the hangover.

RIP
Redser

HANGOVERS

How you treat the morning-after depends on what sort of hangover you've got. And what sort of a hangover you've got depends on what you were drinking.

I don't go much beyond the odd pint of cider these days. Not with my bladder. As it is, I have to sit near the toilets in Foley's and tell Winnie to keep my gangway clear by kicking her leg out occasionally. But when you've been married to Redser, you get to know your hangovers. He was like the Poet Laureate of the morning-after. There was no detail he couldn't describe.

Redser worked out there were five sorts of hangover. He wrote them down in a notebook I still treasure. It's the most beautiful thing he ever did, and it's probably, apart from the kids and that hook he put up for the shed keys, his lasting legacy.

According to Redser's theory, the cheaper the drinks were, the bigger the hangover, and the more expensive the cure.

So, as he said, you may as well drink too much of something nice.

I've refined his theory over time – I've had a couple of hangovers of my own, I won't pretend to be a saint – and here I am, proud to present the fruits of the finest drinking mind Ireland ever produced.

Redser's Hangover Guide

Edition 1.0

5 types

....

THE BASIC

Symptoms:
Headache, slight fuzziness, reluctance to use the bus.

Cause:
Something nice. A wedding. Wine with a fancy label. An evening with a €60 minimum spend these days. The morning-after of the upper crust.

Treatment:
Couple of tablets, fresh air. No more than €1.

....

THE GATHERING STORM

Symptoms:
Headache, dizziness, terrible sense of doom, dry
mouth.

Cause:
Hard liquor. Whiskey, brandy, one of those foreign
ones no one can spell, and anything else off the high
shelf of the bar. Usually around €50 total.

Treatment:
Lie-in, four tablets, beans on toast, coffee. Roughly €3.

....

THE NEVER-AGAIN

Symptoms:
Headache, trouble standing, lack of energy, mouth
like a potato-picker's hands, the feeling everyone's
staring at you, nausea, waking up with half your
clothes on, sweating like Elvis in a greenhouse.

Cause:
Mixing the good with the bad. Pints plus shots. Several
fighting lagers followed by a few silly feckin' things
that hardly touch the sides. €35–40.

Treatment:
Pint of water, four tablets, sausage sandwich, three
coffees, feel miraculously better, chuck the whole lot
back up, back to bed. €12 plus lost earnings from a day
off work.

THE DEATH WISH

Symptoms:
Bollocking headache, double vision, whistling in the ears,
tongue that doesn't fit your mouth lolling about like you've
got a stunned sealion trapped behind your teeth, whole body
stinking like a drip tray, still wearing your trousers (piss
atlas down your trousers), still wearing your shoes, not
convinced your legs are yours, waking up somewhere feckin'
uncomfortable (the bath, a hedge, the bilge of a trawler) and no
idea how you got there.

Cause:
You may not recall exactly. Clues are a half-eaten kebab in
one pocket, a NO FOULING THE FOOTWAY sign ripped off
a lamp-post in the other. Probable cause was a shiteload of
bareknuckle lager. Not the good sort. The stuff that smells
like Elnett and leaves you with an aftertaste like you slept
with your house keys in your mouth. Total spend €25 roughly.
Feckin' roughly.

Treatment:
All the tablets you're allowed (including the ones for people
with broken backs), day off, bleach to get the bathroom back to
normal. €15 and up, plus lost earnings.

THE TORTURE CHAMBER

Symptoms:
Total and overwhelming incapacity, relentless emptying,
no idea what time of day it is – in fact no idea what day it is
or when this started or when the feck it'll ever end – loss of
identity, feeling like you spent three hours bodyslamming a
brick wall, a face like a duff waxwork, a mouth like a dogshit
bin, every inch of you honking like a dead rat in a U-bend full of
blue cheese, the creeping panic that you might have to get your
bungalow adapted, the worry that you might have called a
radio phone-in with some new and unusual opinions last night,
the worry that you may have called your neighbour/child/
priest with some new and unusual opinions last night, sweat
like battery acid burning your top layer of skin away.

Cause:

Again, your memory may be compromised. Things you might find: you've lost your wallet/purse, you've lost your clothes/hair, there's an empty bottle of lighter fluid or a hospital ventilator next to your bed, God. Alcohol you drank almost certainly was shite. Used to be homebrew in Redser's day, but now it's usually Trampagne. You know, that stuff that calls itself cider but has never been within orbiting distance of a feckin' apple. Fizzy industrial gutstripper made from turnip peelings and nail varnish remover, decanted into a wrist-breaking three-litre bottle and labelled Shite Lightning or Frosty Feck's. That stuff. Starts by hurting you, finishes by wiping you out. Mind you, it's fierce cheap. So it's not all bad news. €10.

Treatment:

Nothing is too good for this bastard. Give it everything you've got. You won't be able to get out of bed (or wherever you've collapsed: floor, garden, emergency room) for a day or two, so treat it like recovery from major trauma – which it is. Lie very still, say nothing (except to your solicitor, if you get introduced to him unexpectedly), and wait for it to pass. Try to take your mind off it. Maybe watch that film where the fellow gets trapped and has to hack his own arm off with a pen-knife, if you need a bit of light relief. Or cut your own arm off with a pen-knife, if the film doesn't cheer you up. Forget painkillers and fried food: you can't open a bottle of pills when your hands feel like a pair of iron weights, let alone be trusted with a hob, or a wallet. God knows, you'd need to call the emergency services just to get a packet of crisps open. You'll find that after the first couple of days bits of your body will come back to life. It starts with your eyelids. Sure, nurses are good at interpreting blinks. That fellow wrote a whole bestselling book with blinks. I didn't do this one without a few nods, I can tell you.

SCALDS AND BURNS

The same thing, except one's wet and the other's dry. Treat both with either hot or cold water. Apparently. I was always told to run a burn under a cold tap. Now you're supposed to run it under a hot tap. Obviously, the answer is to get it wet, whether you dip it in snow or pour a boiled kettle over it. But sure, that can't be right. Where's Dr Flynn when you need him?*

Maybe just use some cream. Not the good stuff. The stuff that comes in a squirty can will do. It's pretty cold (or hot, or whatever they want this week).

CUTS

There's almost nothing a Mammy can't mend with a magic kiss. Kissing it better has been a remedy for millions of years. Mind you, depends on the cut. A mouthful of blood is an acquired taste, even for the most seasoned vampire. And obviously, it depends on the size of the cut. If someone's cut their leg off, don't waste valuable time trying to get the stump in your mouth. Call a feckin' ambulance.

SAUCEPAN STUCK ON THE HEAD

Every Mammy's had a little soldier who can't get his tin hat off. I've had a retired veteran who couldn't get his off, that time Grandad went looking for the stopcock because he didn't want his bath. Winnie says a bit of elbow grease and a good tug does the trick, but she says that about a lot of things, the filthy cow. I say get the hammer out, and frighten the creepers out of them. The shock causes them to pull a long face, and the saucepan comes off easier.

FOOT IN A BUCKET

Another common household mishap. There's no way round this one – someone has to grab the bucket and pull like feck. That'll be me, then. And that someone usually ends up flat on her back with a sore arse.

MAMMY'S TIP

A grandad is a good cover for any story. Use him sparingly.

FALLS

You'll sometimes find, as a Mammy, that you end up flat on your back with a sore arse. Say, for instance, just for the sake of, ooh, I don't know, as an example, after pulling a feckin' bucket off Grandad's foot. The dozy thumping great lump.

The best thing for a fall is to lie flat on your back and pull the Mammy's emergency cord: get the family in. They can rally round and run the house for you, while you spend a couple days in bed with a hot water bottle and a pile of magazines.

If you're canny, you'll make sure that you save pulling the bucket off Grandad's foot until there's plenty of washing-up and ironing piling up. That way it all gets magically done while you're recovering.

And if you're super canny, you'll stick a bucket on Grandad's foot any time it gets too much for you. *(To let you into a secret, you don't even have to bother with the bucket. You can just pretend it happened. It's not like Grandad's going to drop you in it. Everything to him is either now or before, so whether it happened five minutes ago or in 1972, it's all the same to him.)*

THE UNMENTIONABLES

There are things that happen to a Mammy of a certain age that don't need going into detail about. Let's just say your trampolining days are over.

None the less, it's worth knowing your limits before you go on a roller-coaster, or take part in a three-legged race.

There's a lot of talk these days about the pelvic flaw. I think it's plain feckin' cruel to call it a flaw. It's not a flaw, it's just something that happens because you've fulfilled your role as a Mammy, and squeezed a few puppies out. That doesn't make you flawed. It feckin' IMPROVES YOU. Kids give you a sense of perspective. They give you a reason to get up in the morning. They give you an excuse to have a headache any time you need one. They're bucking invaluable. Cherish them.

And so what if they change you? What's wrong with that?

You can't carry around a cast-iron shit weighing as much as a cannonball for nearly a year, then pretend it hasn't made a feckin' difference to your fizzique. No one's that big a liar. Well, no woman is.

The bottom line *(and we don't call it that any more, according to our Cathy)* is that there are things that us ladies just COPE with. Men, for instance. We take them in our feckin' stride. And thanks to the chemist's shelves and our good sense not to make a piss-up out of a brewery, we get on with it – without complaint. You could say the same thing about laundry. Or teenagers. Or shortcrust pastry. It's all the same: a cross we have to bear. And like our good Lord, we should bear it with a smile.

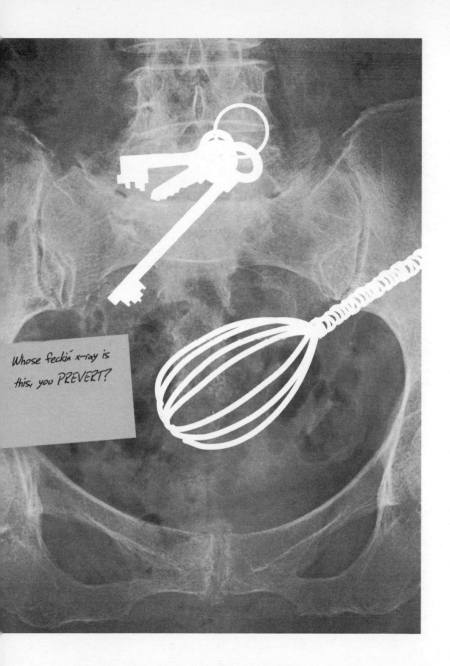

THE DERMOT SCALE

If your nearest and dearest find themselves feeling a bit out of sorts, it's important they can describe their symptoms to you, so you can describe them to Dr Flynn. Bless him, he likes a drink, and can get a bit forgetful, so you might have to repeat yourself for the first half an hour or so.

Our Dermot gets terrible wind. Always has. He once farted a hole in a nappy. He'd bolt down a bottle and I'd end up thumping him for hours. *(He and Buster have a very similar relationship today.)*

Anyway, with him being such a flatulent kiddy, Dermot became a bit of an expert. And when he had to do a biology project for school, he decided to do it all about wind. He'd seen something in a geography book about the different types of wind and how powerful they are, all done in a scale, and he thought it was time there was one for man-made gusts.

He got a D. Best mark he ever had. I'm still that proud of him. We've got this framed in the smallest room *(Grandad's)*.

The Dermot Brown Wind Scale

A scientific experiment by Dermot Brown

Burps	
Basic burp	Enough to get a hard stare from Mammy.
Little ripper	Enough to get a thick ear from Mammy.
Surprise growl	Enough to wake Grandad up. Once he thought he'd had a nightmare about the zoo.
Big ripper	Enough to make people leave the room in disgust. This goes down badly in the doctor's waiting room. CAREFUL: can come with a little bit of vinegary backwash that's a devil to swallow.
Roar	Long enough to say the whole alphabet. Party trick only. Needs a lot of Coke and Monster Munch to come off properly. For the EXPERT only.

Blowoffs	
Party squeaker	Small enough to blame the dog
Trump	You have to say sorry. But it's worth it for the look on their faces
Grunt	The funniest blowoff there is. Brilliant in a car where nobody can get away from it. Doesn't impress girls as much as the fellows.
Settee-shaker	Good for clearing the room if you want to watch the TV. Hangs about a bit in the cushions. Can make plants wilt and net curtains go a bit yellow. Worth having a can of air freshener ready.
Silent poison	DEADLY. Better to run away and make people think there's a dead mouse in the skirting board or Grandad's done a cabbage burp than risk sticking around for the thrashing. Can make Grandad choke, so there's a diversion. STRICTLY NOT FOR UNDER THE COVERS. Would probably kill you in your sleep like one of them broken boilers.

FAMILY
GATHERINGS

Hatches, matches and dispatches: that's what my Mammy used to call family gatherings. And when I'm wafting a lit match through the serving hatch at a wake because Grandad's let off, I think she knew what she was talking about.

There are two sorts of family gathering: one all the family attends, like a nice party, and one all the family attends AND HAS TO BE NICE TO EACH OTHER at, like a wedding or a baptism.

BAPTISMS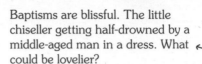

Baptisms are blissful. The little chiseller getting half-drowned by a middle-aged man in a dress. What could be lovelier?

You should be buying something for the little one who's being baptised. Not clothes, because the poor fecker will be done up like one of those toilet roll dollies, whether they're a boy or a girl. But something else: a teddy, a dummy, a silver thing (teddy? dummy?) – something they can keep for the rest of their life and only need to look at once every ten or twenty years when they open the weird box in the loft full of all the stuff from before they can remember anything. *'Who bought me a christening snuffbox?'* That could be you.

I've still got the little bell I was given at my baptism. Feck knows who got me a bell, or what it was for. Perhaps they thought it'd come in handy before I could talk, to get my nappy changed or ask for another bottle, me ringing it like a little Lady summoning her feckin' servants. Or perhaps I had an infant skin condition they thought might develop into something I'd need a bell round my neck for in later life.

And I've still got the miniature silver monkey-wrench Mark got at his baptism. It's a bottle opener, and I knew that then, but it was the thought that counted. Grandad never did buy outside his comfort zone. Mind you, it was that or a keyring with a girl that took her clothes off when you turned it upright, so our Mark got away lightly.

WEDDINGS

The most important family gatherings are weddings. And the biggest thing to decide is WHO'S NOT FECKIN' INVITED. Who IS invited is a piece of cake: it's anyone you can just about stand. You judge a family's standing by how many too many there are at a matching. But there are plenty who don't go on the list. It's good to have a good basic blacklist you can adapt for any occasion.

- ~~Uncle Bill~~ *(gets a bit handy)*

- ~~Buster's family~~ *(the cake will be gone before we've even seen it)*

- ~~The milkman who says he wasn't there~~ *(he was and we know it)*

- ~~Cousin Bellamy the Farmhand~~ *(he sniffs the girls)*

- ~~Anyone from the butcher's~~

- ~~Father Mundy~~ *(his ears are too close together)*

- ~~Stephanie~~ *(the cow)*

- ~~Redmond~~ *(no one knows whose son he is, not even his four mothers)*

- ~~The Tippetts~~ *(they've all got strange thumbs – that can't be right)*

- ~~Terry~~ *(makes funny noises and frightens the kiddies)*

- ~~Young Ciaran Whelan~~ *(could drink the place dry in 20 minutes flat)*

- ~~Hilary~~ *(twat)*

Sometimes you have to have Hilary on the list, though. Especially if it's her daughter getting hitched to my son. Shite. Life deals you these hands, and you have to work out how to cheat the other party out of their winnings. I find it's usually best to lie *(time of ceremony, location of ceremony, who's getting married)* and see what she'll swallow to minimize contact. It's for the greater good.

The Dress

The dress is the biggest thing about the wedding day. Usually literally. I've been to weddings where it looked like half a lace factory was coming down the aisle. Trains longer than the queue at a Daniel O'Donnell concert. If she has the figure for it, better for a bride to wear a slim-cut thing. Nothing tarty, though. There's altogether too much leg coming out at weddings for my liking. The groom's halfway to his honeymoon present by the time she arrives at the altar. Some things are worth waiting for. And you're not supposed to find out whether they're worth waiting for until you've bucking well waited for the feckin' things and it's too late to turn back.

The Cake

This is the second-biggest thing. Again, literally, sometimes. Hilary wanted Maria and Dermot's cake to be seven tiers high. I said, we'll never see the feckin' happy couple behind all that. It'll look like they're hiding. She said we could put them up a stepladder. Feckin' ridiculous. 'Look, there's my son, the 9' groom with his 8' 6" wife climbing their feckin' rich fruit and marzipan skyscraper.' It would have looked like a Delia Smith remake of *King Kong*.

Anyway, she shed a few tears and the cake shed a few tiers. It was three high in the end, and a lovely bit of work, with a little icing Dermot and Maria on the top. *(I caught Hilary trying to trouser them after the do, the feckin' vulture. She was probably going to stick pins in our Dermot. Or bite his head off. I got them in the end. And then the dog did, but that's between you and me. Keep your trap shut, but unless Dermot mentions a ring of bite marks round his stomach, I reckon we've proved voodoo's a load of old shite.)*

The Best Man's Speech

A Mammy needs to keep a feckin' close eye on this. I know what young lads are like, wanting to tell filthy stories and make the groom out to be a wild animal with prison eyes and a permanent feckin' third leg. So make sure none of this gets the mention:

- *Previous marriages*
- *Anyone the bride might have fallen into bed with*
- *Run-ins with the law*
- *Any little accidents*
- *Anything to do with the docks*
- *Hilarious stories about the church*
- *EVERYTHING TO DO WITH MONEY*
- *Things they did for a bet*
- *Things they drank for a bet*
- *Things they ate for a bet*
- *Things they slept with for a bet* (in fact, avoid betting altogether)
- *Breaking into the zoo* (you'd be surprised how often it happens)
- *Anything they tried to smoke* (including banana skins and tea leaves)
- *Novelty underwear*
- *Alleyways and caravans*
- *What they did with the school tortoise*
- *Hilarious driving stories* (it won't have been their feckin' car, and it'll probably have been someone's who's at the wedding)
- *Anything to do with swelling up*
- *Stuff their father told them that you haven't heard before*
- *Holidays in the Greek islands*
- *Any mention of washing it out, talcing it and using it again*
- *Finding themselves in the wrong room*
- *Banjo strings* (says Winnie – feck knows what she's on about – she must go to a lot of feckin' country and western-themed weddings)
- *Anything to do with waking up*
- *Things they added to snowmen*
- *The Welsh*

Ideally, your best man's stories should all take place downstairs, in broad daylight, and in front of at least two trustworthy witnesses. And have a happy ending. And be able to be read out in front of anyone. Anyone. Even a 100-year-old priest with a nervous disposition and perfect hearing. And there should be a few gentle jokes in there too. Something like, *'What did Eve get Adam for his birthday? A World's First Dad mug.'* Sure, there's books full of the feckin' things in the shops. There's probably one next to this book right now. Why haven't you bought this book yet, you feckin' skinflint? Put your hand in your feckin' pocket. It's not like you're going to memorize all this shite.

Stag and Hen Parties

This is one area a Mammy doesn't get involved in. Thank the Lord. Except she feckin' hears about it when one of her sons ends up wearing an adult nappy in a Chinese restaurant and wearing two crispy fried ducks as boxing gloves. So, for feck's sake, get them to FUCK OFF OUT OF TOWN. Preferably the bucking country.

Jaysus, the girls you see wobbling round Temple Bar some nights. They look like they're wearing a load of feckin' Christmas decorations, sound like a slaughterhouse full of piglets, and they're wearing more make-up than Sharon fucking Osbourne gets through in a year. Even the feckin' tramps are embarrassed to be seen around them.

And as for the fellows . . . well, at least they disappear into the mucky clubs. Mind you, you'd think they'd be cold. Sure, even if it's feckin' −30° out there, they're still only wearing shirts. Not tucked in, mind. When did everyone get so hot? Must be that global warming. Perhaps people are born hotter than they were when I was a girl. The only time I ever saw my Redser in his untucked shirt, he was in the bath. And he had a vest on. Christ, that house was like the feckin' Arctic. It's no wonder we didn't need a fridge. We used to warm the place up by leaving the door open.

The Wedding Reception

Hold the reception somewhere nice, but not too fancy. A social club is fine. A carvery, if you want to shell out for something a bit special. Not a hotel. Those places are a feckin' tourist trap. And they make you feel so feckin' guilty about being there. And if you've just spent two hours at a bucking Catholic wedding, with the Lord looking down on your family with one eyebrow raised, the last thing you want is some greasy little gobshite in a penguin suit turning his nose up at you when you ask for a pint of cider to go with your coffee.

And don't put anything too exotic on the menu. People are funny fish when it comes to – well, funny fish, for instance. Prawns. *Prawns frighten the old people.* They think they're going to get food poisoning. And anything with too much garlic in it. You don't want to have to queue for the toilets during the disco. Forget about 'Oops Upside Your Head', it'll be 'Oops Inside Your Legs'.

Mammy's Tip
Get an advance guard of four or five grey-haired guests who can keep the priests talking and away from the provisions until everyone's had at least one mini kiev. They're like black and white wasps round a buffet, the greedy feckers.

You're safe with anything that's 90 per cent pastry. And you can buy pallets of mini-pastries at Iceland. They're easy to heat up, they don't treat your mouth like a science experiment, and they're cheaper than food.

The bulk of your budget should go on DRINK, of course. This is a feckin' wedding, not a detention, and you want to sluice the bride and groom away on honeymoon in style. Get your guests good and merry – then start charging behind the bar. They'll soon fuck off. Except the rich ones. So you set the priests on them. A bit of Church Fund talk usually makes their taxis magically arrive. It's a feckin' miracle. If there's one thing the rich hate more than each other, it's charity.

A Successful Marriage

What can I say? What can little old Mammy tell you about a loving and steadfast union? I'm no expert. But my Redser and I were happily married 'til the day the good Lord served him his conscription papers. Never a cross word. Well, never more than twice a day. Except weekends. If you ask me, I think there's three things that make a successful marriage.

THINGS TO DO WITH PEGS

NO.5 | SILENCER

Works for snoring, talking and swearing. Do not seal both nose and mouth without checking life insurance policies first.

1. _____

Tell your other half you love them every day. Even if they're not in the room. Which is much easier to do, but still counts. I've checked with Father Quinn.

2. _____

Never go to sleep on a bad word. And, if it looks like that's going to happen, and the light's out, and you haven't settled your differences, take a deep breath . . . *and fart on your beloved's leg. It soon puts things into perspective.* And gives you something else to talk about. You'll be back in each other's arms in about three minutes, I guarantee it.

3. _____

Tell each other the truth about everything. And I mean everything. *Every feckin' thing.* Except their breath, obviously. There's no need to be harsh. *(Besides, you get used to it.)* Oh, and their weight. Some things are best left unsaid. And whether they look their age, of course. It pays to be nice, even if it's bending the truth a bit. And what you think of their parents, obviously. And their brothers and sisters, for that matter. And their DIY. And their feet. Jaysus, their feet. And where that godawful necklace they bought you went. And how many glasses of port you've had. And their ear hair. And how you came by all that cheap lamb. And where the savings book is. But otherwise, everything. Without honesty, what is a marriage? Oh, and what you think of their driving.

I knew I shouldn't have boil-washed that bin. It used to be up to my waist.

THE
JOY OF S-E-K-S

BY WINNIE McGOOGAN

S-E-K-S is a beautiful thing between man and wife. Or man and someone else's wife. Or wives.

When the man from the publisher told me he wanted me to cover
the bedroom, I thought he meant toss some dust-sheets over
the divan. Then, when he explained what he meant, I told him,
if you think you're going to get me to write anything rude
or filthy, you can fuck off. Oh, don't think I don't know how
to keep a man happy in the bedroom. Let him put up shelves.
But what goes on upstairs stays upstairs. I might be throwing
myself open in this book, but I think it's important for
everyone to know I still have private parts.

So he's asked Winnie to do it. And may the Lord have feckin'
mercy on the pair of them.   *Mrs A. Brown*

Hello girls. Now, you don't need me to tell you that a bit of fun between the sheets is essential for a loving relationship. And a quiet life. So here's a sort of Korma Sumatra guide to keeping your sex life ticking over nicely.

I tried to pose for some raunchy photos for this with my Jacko, but what with the short visiting hours and him nil-by-mouth, we had trouble getting the best out of some of the positions. So I've asked your man from the book people if someone could draw it like it's me and Daniel O'Donnell. There's eight different positions here – one for each night of the week.

The Monday
The good old Adam and Eve. Eve lies back, like the lady of luxury she is, while Daniel does all the hard work.

The Tuesday
The Adam and Eve again, maybe with a bit less oomph. A girl can get exhausted, you know.

The Wednesday

...ve's back is starting to play up. Sure, I'm only ...eing realistic. Even Daniel O'Donnell doesn't ...ave healing powers.

The Thursday

Poor Daniel. Look at him. There's only so many stairs a man can run up before he's out of puff. What he needs is a nice cup of tea.

The Friday

...'s been a long week. Poor Eve's taken ... battering these last few nights, and Daniel ...ust be wishing he had a Stannah stairlift ... get him up the last few flights.

The Saturday

Good news. Eve's found the stairlift!

The Sunday

...unday is ...aditionally a ...ay of rest.

The Birthday

This is for special occasions, though you can get away without it at Christmas if you give him enough booze during the day. (I used to spike my Jacko's chestnuts.)

Sure, it'd be nice to have a lovely unspoilt picture of the whole family in here somewhere

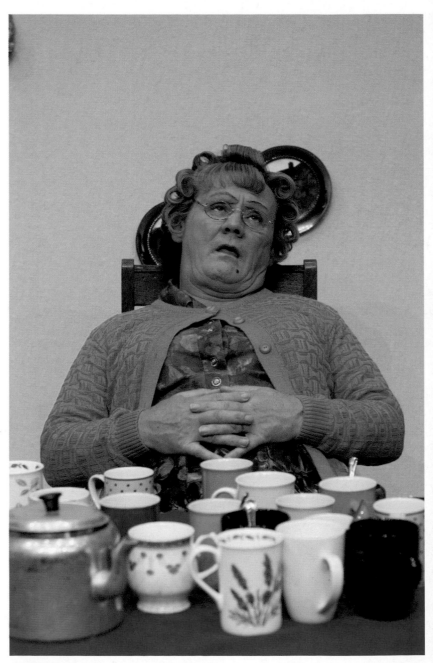

When I'm exhausted after a long day's tea drinking, I like to relax with a nice cup of tea.

WAKES

When your time is done on this good earth, your time is done. You don't get any curtain calls or second chances. As a wise fellow once said, life is not a rehearsal. Good job, too, because I'd be asking if I could come back for the show when everyone had got their shite together and stopped crashing into each other and fucking up their lines.

Man has but a short time to live. Woman usually has a bit longer. A lot longer, in my case. So you've to make the most of it. Spread a little happiness. A lot, if you've a big enough knife and a good wrist. You don't know how long you've got, so be nice to each other. My Redser used to take the piss a lot, especially when I nagged him about his health. I told him, there's no need to be cruel. He'd be there, with his whiskey and his sarky bloody comments and his Embassy King Size, like he was Cyril feckin' Fletcher. I used to say to him, you'll be laughing on the other side of your face when you have a stroke.

He might have been a silly arse, but at least he lived his life and loved his life. At least he made his mark. You knew he'd been there. And he had a feckin' ball. So should we all.

GRANDAD BROWN c. 2013

Look at Grandad. Slumped in his armchair, saying feck all, not even bothering to bother anybody, barely noticed *(except when he's been at the pickled onions)*. He's little more these days than a feckin' cushion with false teeth. What would you rather be? A pillow or a pillock? Exactly.

Where was I?

Wakes. That was it. Ah, Jaysus, if a wake isn't the best and worst of everything. It's like cod liver oil ice cream. Make the most of it, though. Your dearly departed wouldn't want you to stand around blubbing like a feckin' *X Factor* contestant while everyone solemnly trapped on about what a good soul he or she was. They'd be saying *have a party.* And they'd be right.

Nothing is too much fun for a wake. Except balloon animals, to be fair. They didn't go down at all well at Eamonn Madden's wake. Especially the giraffe, what with Eamonn having met his maker after falling off the boom of that orange crane. Terrible tragedy. Mind you, it was a feckin' foolish place to go for New Year's.

Come to think of it, there's a few things you shouldn't try at a wake.

- • **HIDE AND SEEK**
- • **MUSICAL CHAIRS**
- • **MURDER IN THE DARK**
- • **DEAD LIONS**
- • **CLUEDO**
- • **AEROBICS**
- • **SWINGBALL**

But there's plenty you can do.

- • The Conga

- • Bridge/Pontoon/Twenty-five/ Snap *(just for matchsticks, obviously)*

- • Charades *(but avoid things like The Departed)*

- • Pin the Tail on the Donkey

- • Singalongs *(nothing too dreary, no Sting)*

- • Consequences *(unless your loved one got caught in a nasty accident)*

- • Guess Who? *(unless there's one who looks like your loved one)*

In short, give them a good spread *(sandwiches will do. And remember, the smaller you cut them, the more they'll think they've eaten – I get mine down to the size of stamps)* and a good drink or two *(maybe just the one)* and keep the door open, so it looks like it's never too early to leave. There'll always be one who's still hanging around when you're the last one standing, and in your dressing-gown at that. Some people can't take a hint, Father Pisshead Finnissy.

Feel free to put up dignified decorations, but avoid anything garish. You might think the stuff down the shops is all a bit sombre, but don't be tempted to grab something more colourful; it might look less appropriate when it's up. Noreen Traynor, God love her, could never read very well, and when her Willie died, put up some bunting that read 'Congratulations you've passed'. No one had the heart to mention it.

EASTER

Easter's a bit like Christmas. It's mainly for the kiddies. There's absolutely nothing for the grown-ups at Easter, except a lot of feckin' cooking and baking to do. I always do a Simnel cake – and buy twice as much marzipan as I need, because I find about half of it tends to disappear while I'm rolling it out. All those off-cuts have to go somewhere, and there's usually nobody looking. I smell so much of almonds by Easter Sunday, my breath can send someone with nut allergy into prophylactic shock.

You'll be needing an egg hunt, of course. If you're buying one of those big eggs that comes in a box the size of a feckin' van with a free mug and about 40 gallons of fresh air wrapped in plastic, good luck to you.

I prefer buying a few smaller ones, so the kiddies have a bit more to do. Otherwise, they find one egg, looming out of the shrubbery like a feckin' Mayan temple, and Easter's over in about five minutes.

Sure, you want them to think the Easter Bunny made a bit of a feckin' effort. The tooth fairy wouldn't leave an IOU. *(Although Redser once told Mark the tooth fairy was on strike, like any good socialist. Mark wanted to know what she'd done with his tooth. Redser said she'd probably burned it on a brazier on the picket line. That caused a few tears.)*

Don't hide Easter eggs places the kiddies will think of first, like the cupboards and your bag. Try places like the bin and the washing machine. Winnie once forgot to buy any eggs and told Sharon the Easter Bunny must have hidden them on the bus. Couple of months the poor girl spent rootling around under people's seats every time she rode into town.

THINGS TO DO WITH PEGS
NO.8 | EASTER BUNNY TOY

And that's Easter sorted too.

HALLOWEEN

The colcannon's on the hob, the barnbrack's made, and there's a tub of apples ready for bobbing. That can mean only one thing: you've made far too much bucking effort. Grab a cup of tea and a sharp knife, and have some fun. It's time to carve the pumpkin.

Aren't there some artistic pumpkins out there nowadays? Winking ones, ones with moustaches and surprised looks. Still, you can't beat an old-fashioned lookalike. Here's how I carve mine.

---

1. *Take a knife and cut a lid in the top of the pumpkin.*

---

2. *Spoon out the stuff that looks like sick.*

---

3. *Sit Grandad next to your pumpkin.*

---

4. *Copy him.*

A couple of those in the window and you'll weed out all but the hardiest trick-or-treaters.

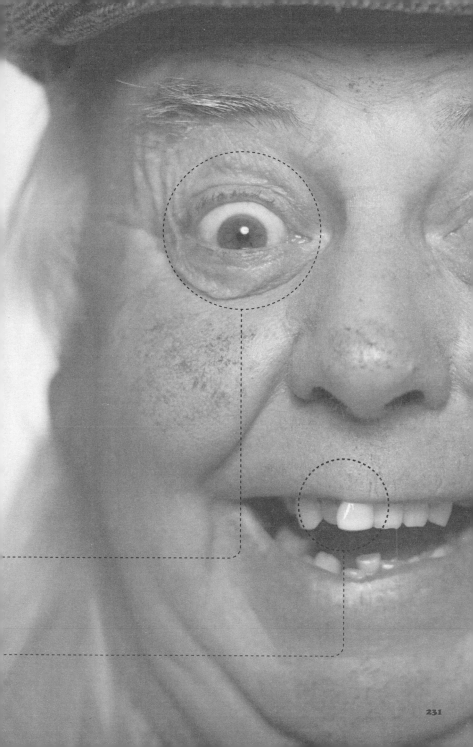

How to Deal with Trick-or-treaters

Ah, there's nothing quite as heartwarming as a couple of chisellers coming to the door all dressed up as skeletons or Ben feckin' 10 or whatever it is Bono's always on about, asking you, 'Trick or treat, lady?'

Bless their little cotton socks. You can always send the little so-and-sos away with a sweetie or two, of course. But where's the fun in that? It's not often some kiddies give you a feckin' open goal. Enjoy yourself.

Mammy's Tip
Don't throw away cobwebs. They make ideal Halloween decorations.

- Say 'I'll have a treat, thanks,' and start helping yourself to the stuff they've collected in their buckets.

- Answer the door in a bloody pinafore, holding a meat cleaver, twitching.

- Say, 'Just a minute, lads, I'll find you something,' shut the door, and when they finally ring the bell again send Cathy back to answer it. Cathy says, *'What?'* When the kiddies mention the old lady went to get some sweeties, get Cathy to say, *'The old lady? But she died twenty years ago . . .'* Kids can scarper pretty bucking fast when they think the walking dead are around.

- Get Grandad to answer the door. Like I said, kids scarper pretty fast when they think the walking dead are around.

CHRISTMAS

Nollaig shona! Christmas is the big fecker, and needs a lot of preparation.

I start getting ready for Christmas just after Christmas. There's a lot you can do in the bit between Boxing Day and New Year: wrapping up the presents you didn't want that you can give to someone else next year, cutting up the used wrapping paper and making new decorations out of it for next year, cutting up the cards and making gift tags out of them for next year, cutting up the blouse Hilary bought you and making dog rags from it – and, of course, finishing off all the chocolates hanging round the back of the tree that no fecker found and that I put there as a little extra something for Mammy.

Decorations

You can never have too many decorations. Any self-respecting home at Christmas should look like Liberace's broken in and gone postal with a glitter gun.

If your house is anything like mine *(the size of a normal feckin' house, Hilary, not your sugary great palace with its 'family wet room' or whatever the weird bucking hell it's called)* you'll need the following:

- **Tree** – one big fecker

- **Tinsel** – about half a mile of the stuff

- **Baubles** – no more than 500

- **Angel** – a homemade one will do; mine's the top half of a Barbie glued into a toilet roll tube and sprayed gold

- **Lights** – about a mile of the things

- **Bits and pieces for the sideboard**
  – a bit of spare tinsel round the photo frames is good enough for me

- **A wreath for the front door**

If you can be arsed to get a **nativity scene**, you go ahead. We had one, but Grandad ate the manger, thinking it was a stale Double Decker. Then someone tripped over the stable, and one of the wise men lost his head. Plus the donkeys never looked that convincing, if you ask me. No donkey I've ever seen has horns. I think they resprayed a job lot of goats. Perhaps they don't have donkeys in Taiwan. Oh, and the wiring in the halos got hot and Joseph's head melted. It was less the Birth of Our Lord than the end of *Raiders of the Feckin' Lost Ark*.

Don't bother buying a real **holly wreath** for the front door. They only last about three weeks and they'll set you back half a bucking turkey if you're not careful. Redser made ours, and it's still in use today. It's the tyre from a wheelbarrow with a load of varnished bayleaves pinned round it. Lovely bit of work it is, so.

Christmas Dinner

To any Mammy, Christmas dinner is THE BIG ONE. The trophy. The highlight of her year. The thing the family remembers her for, for at least a couple of hours, anyway. And like all big events *(weddings, childbirth)* it's a PAIN IN THE CRACK. The mother of all pains in the crack, in fact. But it's worth it just to see the exhausted looks on their faces when they finish.

Don't let anyone tell you any other way: Christmas is a time for overeating. And you can't expect to overfeed a load of mouths unless you make far too much food. Money should be no object: start saving in February. Put a little by every week. This meal is going to be your magnum opus *(or 'big ice cream')*.

The important thing is that, for one meal, and one meal only, you completely forget about the normal size of the human stomach. Look at what you'd dish up any other day of the year – couple of boiled spuds, three sossies, puddle of peas – the meal they'll pat their tums after and sigh, 'Ah! I'm right full, Mammy. Off down the pub . . .' Now triple or quadruple it – three times as much meat, eight times as many potatoes – and serve it up without warning. It's an act of maternal aggression, as if you've had some sort of brain seizure that made you look at your children round the table, already slightly full of Christmas tree chocolate, and mistake them for a school

of hungry baleen whales, or a row of steam train furnaces, gaping open for great shovel loads of fuel. Eat! Eat! Eat!

The key word is 'trimmings'.

You hear people talk about 'all the trimmings' – and they mean roast potatoes, parsnips, carrots, stuffing and the like. That's not all the trimmings, that's three or four of the trimmings.

This is the bare minimum that should be on all their plates:

Turkey breast

Turkey leg

Sage and onion stuffing

Forcemeat

Sausages

Potatoes

Parsnips

Carrots

Sprouts

Red cabbage

White cabbage

Greens

Gravy

Bread sauce

Cranberry sauce

That's the minimum. The least of the feast. Really, you should also have:

Pigs in their blankets

Roast ham

Chestnut and prune stuffing

Mashed potatoes
(as well as roast, not instead of)

Swede

Turnip

Cauliflower cheese

Peas

Redcurrant jelly

And if you're doing the job properly and don't want the family going hungry, you'll want to be serving them all this too:

Roast beef

Boiled potatoes
(as well as mashed and roast)

Potato stuffing

Potato farls

Popovers

Pease pudding

Roast garlic

Curly kale

Apple sauce

Pickled walnuts

Pickled onions (Grandad)

Crisps

Now that, my friend, is what ALL the feckin' trimmings look like. Best to keep the extra big plates for this sort of meal. Mark's even reinforced the kitchen table for me with a couple of offcuts of steel joist he came by.

Don't forget the drink, of course: mulled wine (tip: you can get away with Ribena and brandy), and Guinness for the kiddies.

And when they've made a hole in that lot, there's the afters. This is my typical second course.

Plum pudding
(served with flaming brandy)

Christmas cake (full of whiskey)

Trifle (full of sherry)

Cider loaf

Mince pies (full of brandy)

Baked apples (with plenty of brandy)

Pear crumble
(don't skimp on the brandy)

Brandy sauce

Rum sauce

Brandy butter

Rum butter

Brandy snaps

Liqueur chocolates

And don't forget the drink. Brandy, rum, sherry or whiskey are best. Or a nice liqueur. It's the time of year you throw the doors of the drinks cabinet open and let that cobwebbed bottle of ouzo come blinking into the light. There must be something you can pour it into! (Gravy, festive cocktail, Grandad.)

And you can follow it with something a little stronger, if you get my meaning. (Don't be coy. You know exactly what I'm feckin' on about. The sort of thing you have to ask around for. Somebody always knows somebody. If you're stuck, ask for One-Eyed Whatsisname. There's usually a One-Eyed Somebody in town, and he usually lost half his sight in pursuit of the noble distiller's art. You'd think with all this Buy Local stuff that the One-Eyeds would have their own TV series by now.)

There'll always be some smart-arse who asks for cheese and biscuits at this point. Like you'd waste good money on a cheeseboard when there's trimmings to be stocking up on. So keep some packets of Mini Cheddars handy. They're easy to throw and can cause a fair black eye if you chuck them hard enough.

Christmas games

After dinner, if anyone's still awake and able to move, you might like to play a game. Something like Pass The Washing-Up or Mammy Sits It Out. You'll be fucking lucky.

When they do come round, after you've finished the first two or three hours of washing-up, and probably got the cutlery mostly out of the way, here's a few things you can do to liven up the evening.

CHARADES

Everyone takes it in turns to try to remember that film with that fellow in it – you know the one – the one who used to be in that detective thing on the TV. With the girl. You know the girl – she was in the pop charts once with that song. You know the song – the one from the musical. You remember. God, this ouzo's fair strong, isn't it?

TWENTY-FIVE

Everyone counts their empty after-dinner mint wrappers. The winner is the first to twenty-five.

THE RIZLA GAME

Buster comes round and he and Dermot go out in the yard for a smoke. Maria thinks she can smell something funny and goes out and gives them both an almighty bollocking. Dermot loses.

HOT WATER PICTIONARY

One of the fellows thinks there's something wrong with the hot water and they all have a look at the boiler and start drawing diagrams of the pipes, with things like MAINS and RETURN written on them. The winner is the one who gives up trying to decipher Redser's plumbing first.

PICTIONARY

Grandad has to draw a thing. The rest of the family have up to three Christmases to work out what it is, by which time he's forgotten. Actually, he's forgotten after the first ten minutes. And by a quarter of an hour he's forgotten he's playing the bucking game. And he's probably forgotten it's Christmas, too. Years of fun for all the family.

GUESS WHO?

Mammy gets the photo album out, with all the pictures of Mark's and Trevor's and Dermot's ex-girlfriends cut out of it, and the family has to sit around trying to remember who the girl was, and why the two of them split up. Bonus points if you know where they are now, and double bonus if you know what their husbands are doing time for.

SNAP

Everyone takes it in turns to try to get out of the chair they're in. The winner is the one whose bones make the most noise.

CUP OF TEA?

Mammy asks the question to the 'jury' and the jury has to reach a verdict. To begin with, perhaps two of them will. Then it's up to the others to debate the issue until there's a unanimous show of hands for tea. A majority won't do. Playing time: upwards of an hour.

THE JANUARY SALES

Now, I like a bargain as much as the next Mammy, but if you think I'm queuing on the pavement overnight to pick up a cheap sofa, you're a couple of sausages short of a breakfast.

Our Rory's done it, though. He sat in a line from the night before to get into the shops when they opened for the sales. Couldn't find anything he liked, but he had to buy some dry clothes to replace the sopping wet ones he'd slept in. And Sharon did it one year. Silly moo didn't realize the hairdresser's didn't have a January sale. She was the one who fell for that 'buy one get one free' offer they had on haircuts too without reading the small print. Only redeemable by the same customer within seven days.

By the time she'd cashed in the voucher, she looked like Sinead O'Feckin' Connor.

Mammy's Tip

If you know someone with an eye for a bargain, let them do your shopping. Buster Brady goes down the charity shops for me sometimes and it's amazing what some people throw out. I've no idea why anyone would want to get shot of half a dozen bottles of Jameson's with big plastic whatnots clamped round the top, but it made Christmas presents easy that year.

Unidentified
frying object

241

FINAN€ES

A lot of women let their husbands look after the purse strings, because they don't want money worries. But if your husband's got a purse, it's not feckin' money you should be worrying about.

Redser was hopeless with money. He might as well have got paid in ice. We always had more money going out than coming in. The thing is, Redser didn't know the meaning of the word frugal. Or parsimonious. Or balustrade. And I reckon it was failing that verbal reasoning test that meant he could never get a decent job.

He didn't spend the money on himself. He was always splashing out on the weak and the needy. I don't mean like some hooligan pissing on a tramp, but if he saw a sad, pathetic wretch with no hope at all, he'd reach deep in his pocket and hand over the last of his hard-earned cash without a thought. And then watch the fecker limp over the line at the back of the pack at 50-1.

But since Redser left this world, I've had to look after the family finances myself, and I've learned a few things.

In times of no money, it's the love that keeps you together. And if you had no love, sure all the money in the world wouldn't make you happy. I look at the rich, with all their jewellery and their fast cars and their holidays in feckin' ski resorts, and I think, 'Have you got what I've got?' And then I look at my home and think, 'No. You haven't. You've almost certainly got a more expensive hoover, for a feckin' start. Not that you'd know, because you've probably never touched a hoover in your life.'

Remember: money can't buy you love. But if you're buying love, try to remember that's money the kids probably need for shoes.

This chart may come in handy:

IMPORTANT

- Bills
- Rent
- Food
- Clothes

LESS IMPORTANT

- Dial-a-Dick

I taught all of my lot the value of money. By not giving them any. Jaysus, have you seen the pocket money people hand over these days? You'd think the chisellers had them at gunpoint. That's no way to teach them about life. Make the little bollixes earn it. There's always chores that can be done for money. I used to make Dermot clean the car. And then drive it back to where he'd nicked it from.

SAVING MONEY

The whole purpose of this book is to tell you about saving yourself time and money. The sharper a Mammy you are, the cheaper things become. But here are a few canny ways to keep those pennies in your purse, every one of which will make you glad you bought this book.

€ Don't buy new books.

With the popular ones – particularly if they're tied in to television programmes – the silly feckers at the publishers get overexcited and print way too many. Wait a month or two and the bargain bookshops are full of them, shovelled out of skips at knock-down prices. If you paid more than a couple of quid for this book, for instance, they saw you feckin' coming.

€ Are you sure you can't make some things yourself?

With a little imagination, how hard can it be to come up with homemade versions of fish fingers, cornflakes, ketchup and sanitary protection? And be flexible. If it doesn't work as one, try it as another.

THINGS TO DO WITH PEGS

NO.7 | HUNGRY HUNGRY PEGS

Homemade version of the popular and expensive hippo game.

€ Buy in bulk. Take advantage of buy-one-get-one-free offers, particularly if you use something regularly, but beware of buying things you don't need.

Avoid buy-one-get-one-free-offers on:
– Front doors
– Funerals
– Those big wooden Christmas nativity scenes
– Fitted kitchens
– Hysterectomies
– Goats

€ Holiday at home. Instead of jetting off for an expensive holiday, cheer yourself up by booking a Ryanair flight somewhere closer, for under fifty Euros, then just stay at home. Every precious moment you spend not being manhandled and demeaned by those feckers will make you feel like a million dollars.

€ Quality is important, so make savings elsewhere rather than going for budget versions of household standbys. Your family will really taste the difference if you avoid buying knock-down fish fingers, cornflakes, ketchup or sanitary protection.

€ Make a shopping list and stick to it. If you're really struggling, try tearing the shopping list in half to prioritize the important items. (Important: tear it horizontally, not vertically, or you'll waste money and time shopping for fish fin, toilet pap and bicarbonate of sod.)

€ Don't waste leftovers. Eat them.

€ Old socks make perfectly good mittens. And old mittens make perfectly good slippers. And old slippers make pretty good bird-feeders.

€ DIYFS is a great way to save money. Do It Your Feckin' Self. It's not hard to slap on a lick of paint or replace a windowpane that a camera's gone through. It gets a bit tougher with the old electrics, though. You've got to know your browns and your blues

from your blacks and your reds. If in doubt, wire it up and ask Grandad to turn it on. If he goes bright blue and starts dancing the Charleston, you've done something wrong.

€ Take up a money-saving hobby. For instance, saving money. That's a hobby that can save you feckin' hundreds of quid if you really throw yourself into it.

€ Don't buy jigsaws for Grandad. Wait until a plate gets broken, then set him on it with a tube of glue.

€ Don't throw away old lettuce leaves. They make excellent emergency toilet paper. And vice versa.

€ Saying 'no' can save money. When a child's screaming the sweet shop down, you might not want to refuse them that bar of chocolate, but those little treats add up. Remember: if you'd said 'no' a few years ago, rolled over and gone back to your Maeve Binchy, the problem wouldn't even feckin' be there.

€ **Save money on home insurance by not having anything worth replacing.**

€ **Theatre tickets can be very expensive, but you can save a fortune if you watch television.**

€ **The early bird catches the worm.** So be first in the queue when the doctor's surgery opens, and you can peel all the free perfume and hand cream samples out of the magazines in the waiting room.

€ **Water down fruit juice.** And Grandad's beer.

€ **Get EVERY COUPON.** Arrange them in alphabetical order, so you can find what you need quickly. I've got three scrapbooks full of them. I reckon I could get 10c off a feckin' nuclear weapon.

€ **Save water.** They say you can save water by putting a brick in the cistern of your toilet. BE CAREFUL. I thought they were being nice when they were calling it 'a brick'. Took me ten minutes to get sat on the cistern, and I nearly did myself an injury on

the ballcock. Plus the cleaning afterwards was a feckin' nightmare with the thing filling up every time I went to grab my 'brick'. FORGET IT.

PAPERWORK

LETTERS

With all the mail that arrives for a growing family, sometimes it's tempting to let it pile up, but make sure you open any letters that fall on your mat every day, or at least once a week, even ones addressed to you.

The most efficient way to open an exciting-looking letter addressed to another family member is to hold it over a kettle until the glue loosens on the envelope. Then read the contents and reseal. Try not to let them know that you've read their letter. As Maggie Geraghty found out, bursting into tears when your sister mentions Christmas plans will only send up the signal that you've read their test results before they have.

Mammy's Tip

Don't take the freshly steamed stamps from a family member's letter and hand them to their child as 'a gift from Granny'. That's a dead giveaway.

MAIL FROM THE BANK

A bank statement is nothing to worry about. Don't forget: it's only numbers and numbers can't hurt you. Unless you're Toxic O'Farrell who ran the Roxy back in the day, and you've not properly secured the marquee lettering for that 10CC concert. Poor fella.

Check your bank statement for simple errors, for instance, the simple error of spending too much feckin' money on shite. Any unusually large amounts of money going out of your account can be double-checked against your calendar – where were you that night? – or against your drinks cabinet, provided you've taken the precaution of dating and marking the fluid level in the bottles. It usually works out at €30 per quarter-inch of spirits, if I've had the telly shopping on.

But banks do love to write to customers. Don't let them feel lonely. Write back.

Mrs Brown

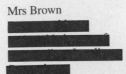

BERKSHIRE & HUNT BANK
145 Parkfields Parade
Killarney St. Dublin D3

10 May 2013

Account number: ▓▓▓▓▓▓▓

Dear Mrs Brown,

According to our records, your account is overdrawn by the sum of €765.80. The arranged overdraft facility for this account is €750.00. Consequently you are currently €15.80 over your agreed limit.

Unfortunately, in light of this situation, we have been forced to levy an unauthorized borrowing fee of €40, to cover our expenses. In addition, there is a standard charge of €20 for this letter. Both sums will be deducted from your account within two working days.

Please make appropriate arrangements to balance your account and settle this matter promptly. If you have problems making repayments, please do feel free to contact us during normal office hours to discuss alternative arrangements.

Yours sincerely,

Michael Fitzmaurice
Escalations Manager,
Berkshire & Hunt Client Interactions

FAO: Michael Fitzmaurice
Berkshire & Hunt Bank
145 Parkfields Parade
Killarney Street
Dublin D3

12 May 2013

Hello there, Mike,

How you doing?

Thanks for letting me know I've spent too much money.
The weight of them bags getting off the bus, I could
have told you that. Last time my back was in that much
pain was my wedding night, pardon my frankness. I put it
out turning the mattress after himself wet it from all
the free Guinness.

Now, you're right that I didn't have that money in the
account, but it'll be back there in a few days when
I've jiggled some cash about. Could you not be patient?

Seems to me you're working awfully fast. I didn't notice that money gone, and I've only got a few hundred.
You've got loads. How did you notice you were fifteen
euro short? I reckon that whoever you've got watching
your balance sheet like a hawk, you could probably stand
to let them take the odd afternoon off. If you're paying them by the hour, that's a saving right there.

Also, €20 for a letter? Whoever's doing your post,
they're paying way over the mark for stamps. I got a
book of twelve for €7. I've sent a birthday present to
New Zealand for less than that, and it was some weight.

Maybe the person who licked the envelope charges a fortune for their time. Do you employ George Clooney to do
it? That would be a reasonable explanation. Otherwise,
where's that €20 going?

Hang on. Is it the paper the letter was written on?
I can't think of any paper that costs €20 a sheet except a €20 note. Maybe you could write the letters
on bank notes in future, and then I could use that
banknote to pay off the overdraft. Do you have a suggestion box?

What I'm saying is if you're splashing out €20,
don't send a letter: get your money's worth. How
about filling a jiffy bag up and enclosing a little
gift to soften the blow? A souvenir piggy bank or a
nice meat pie.

Anyway now, here's a thing.

I have another account with you, you'll remember,
for savings, and I can't help noticing that this
other account is €145.63 in credit.

Now, that's money that you owe me.

So, this is me writing to you to inform you that
you are €145.63 in debt. Unless you take steps to
remedy this situation, I will be writing to you
daily to inform you of the fact. You've shown me
it's important not to let these things slip.

This letter has, unfortunately, cost €40. I know
it's expensive, but it's much longer than yours
and I had to make it up, rather than get it out
of a file, which took a while. Time is money, as
I'm sure you understand. Plus, there are obviously
extra expenses incurred while you remain €145.63 in
the red with me. How about we say €50 for that?

So that's €90, minus the €75.80 I'm short with you.
Let's call it a nice, round €15 you owe me. Pop
it round and we'll all be square. I'll take it in
change. I always need coins for the trolleys.

Or you could post it to me. Now you know what
stamps cost it'll be a snip.

Have a grand one,

Mrs A. Brown

Agnes Brown (Mrs)
Senior Household Manager

**They don't know who they're dealing with. The one thing I've got
is time . . .**

BILLS

Bills need to be dealt with promptly. It's all a matter of efficient filing. As soon as you receive a demand, file it behind the microwave. When the microwave has been pushed dangerously near the edge of the kitchen worktop, it is time to deal with the bills.

Remove any bills that aren't red. Don't panic. Bills are like traffic lights: it's only ignoring the red ones that's dangerous. Non-red bills are only sent by companies as a way of keeping postmen busy now everybody's using the e-mailing and the twitbook.

You can do everything by direct debit, but that can be a nasty surprise if you're not expecting a payment to go out. I like to know when the money's leaving my account *(before we get cut off is usually best)*.

When money's tight, run a tight ship to match. Make sure the whole family knows they're in this together, and reinforce the point by making 'this' the bath. Don't worry about being unpopular. Nobody elects a Mammy. You're in the job for life. It's like North Korea.

There are always ways to get your bills down.

WATER

- Install a water meter. Alternatively, stand near taps, tutting.

- Reuse bathwater – either for baths or, strained and boiled, for tea.

- Only flush the toilet for solids. Put asparagus in the family's food and tell visitors the bathroom's charming smell is 'herbal potpourri'.

ELECTRICITY

- Turn off the TV. Try only watching programmes you don't like, you'll be surprised how much pleasure you can get turning it off.

- Unplug your toaster when it's not in use. In my house, this could save up to forty minutes of toaster power a day.

- Don't let Winnie charge her batteries round your place. No idea why she needs so many.

- Install dimmer switches on all lights, including fridge.

Winnie

- Leave the heating off and put on an extra jumper. And if you're having S-E-K-S, make him wear an extra condom.

- Insulate your loft. Piles of old shite and magazines and bags of baby clothes are good.

- Don't reheat food in the oven. Cook it to double the usual temperature in the first place so it's still hot when you need it later.

- Fit double-glazing to windows, doors and spectacles.

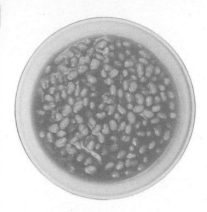

PHONE

- Only talk at length on incoming calls. For example, get the pizza people to phone you back before specifying your order.

- To tell the time, transfer the time from the speaking clock to your mantelpiece clock and then put the phone down.

- Tell your family that any one of them who moves further away than Kerry is 'dead to you'.

- Ban phone sex. Turn off the 'vibrate' function to avoid temptation.

FLUTE OF THE MONTH CLUB

- Sure, it was a tempting offer from the back of the Sunday paper, but do you really need to complete your collection of historically significant miniature porcelain flutes? Cancelling your subscription could free up valuable funds.

FILLING IN FORMS

Sometimes it seems like my life is mainly filling in forms. Cathy says everyone does this in-line nowadays, but I'm not queuing up to fill in a feckin' form. People must be idiots.

From the cradle to the grave, it's non-stop shite that needs to be recorded, applied for, certified and feckin' stamped. I'm surprised they don't beep the feckin' babies when they come out and give you a receipt. There'll be barcodes on their umbilicals next.

When Redser passed over, it was nothing but forms, forms, forms. I could have saved money on the funeral by burying him in feckin' paperwork.

Don't be afraid of a form. I must have done hundreds in my time, and the family are always after me to fill one in for them. To give you an idea, here's one I did for Dermot after he and Buster had a little prang.

IRISH

Cork • Dublin • Aghabullogue

we're behind you

Dear Policyholder,

We have received your Notification. Please complete this form fully and return it to the Company as soon as possible. Please note that the issue of this form is not an admission of liability on the part of the Company.

Upon receipt of your completed form, we will appoint a dedicated representative to manage all aspects of your claim.

Under the conditions of your policy, you must tell us about any incident which may or may not give rise to a claim. Making or attempting to make a fraudulent claim is a criminal offence.

The Company is a member of the Irish Insurance Federation.

Insured

Name: DERMOT BROWN

Policy No: 165589210366N

Address: ~~[redacted]~~

Postcode:

Business or Occupation (incl. Part-time Occupations):
CHARITABLE WORK OUT OF THE GOODNESS OF HIS HEART

Phone No. Home: | Work:
Email: BREAKINANDENTERIN4988@TOPMAIL.IE

Vehicle

Name: DERMOT'S CAR   Model: FRONT: FORD, BACK: DIFFERENT FORD   Cubic Capacity: FECK KNOWS

Year of Manufacture: FRONT: 2002, BACK: 2004   Registration Number: FRONT: 97-D-46778, BACK: HOT SEX

Describe Fully the Purpose for which the Vehicle was being used at the time of the Accident:
DRIVING ORPHANS TO CHOIR PRACTICE

Nature of Goods being carried, if any: ORPHANS, BIBLES, HYMNBOOKS ETC

Driver

Name of Driver: `B U S T E R   B R A D Y`

Date of Birth: 17-08-1989

Address: ▬▬▬▬▬▬▬▬▬▬▬

Postcode:

Business or Occupation (incl. Part-time Occupations): *HELPING THE WEAK, POOR AND NEEDY, LIKE BATMAN*

Phone No. Home: | | | | | | | | | | | Work: | | | | | | | | | |

Was the Driver Injured? Yes ☑ No ☐

If 'YES' What is the Nature of His/Her Injuries: *TWISTED ANKLE RUNNING AWAY, BLOW TO HEAD FROM DERMOT*

Type of Licence Held: Full/Provisional *PROVISIONAL*

Has He/She ever been Convicted of a Motoring Offence? *SHITLOADS* Yes ☑ No ☐

Does He/She own a Motor Vehicle? Yes ☑ No ☐

If 'Yes' state the Name of the Insurers Policy No. *NOT INSURED AS SUCH*

Has He/She been Involved in an Accident within the past five years? *FIVE MINUTES MORE LIKE* Yes ☑ No ☐

If 'Yes' please Give Details: *VARIOUS CRASHES WHILE MAKING GETAWAY FROM SCENE OF CHARITABLE GOOD DEEDS*

Insured Vehicle

Give Full Particulars of Damage to your Vehicle: *REAR NEARSIDE SMASHED TO SHITE BY POLICE CAR, FRONT STOVED IN BY SHOP WINDOW FRAME*

Have you obtained an Estimate for the Repairs? Yes ☑ No ☐

If 'YES' what is the Amount? € *NIALL FROM THE ARCHES SAYS IT'S A WRITE OFF*

Name of Proposed Repairers: *NIALL FROM THE ARCHES*

Address: `T H E   A R C H E S`

When and Where can the Vehicle be Inspected: *IT'S HANGING OUT THE FRONT OF KENEALLY'S PAWN SHOP*

Third Party Property

Name of Third Party(ies): T H E   P O L I C E

Address(es): T H E   P O L I C E   S T A T I O N

Reg. No. of Vehicle (if applicable): *NO FECKIN' IDEA*   Name of Insurers: *POLICE INSURANCE?*

Address: 9 9 9   L E T S B E   A V E N U E ?

Policy No: *DIDN'T SEE THEIR BADGES*

Details of Damage to Third Party Vehicle(s):
FRONT DONE IN AND ALL SMOKE COMING OUT, NEE-NAW LIGHTS SMASHED

Details of Damage to Third Party Property (other than Vehicle(s)):
KENNEALLY'S WINDOW TOTALLY BOLLIXED

Other Details:

Did the Police take Particulars?   *NO. DERMOT AND BUSTER LEGGED IT (TO SAVE ORPHANS)*

Have the Police issued a 'Notice of Intention to Prosecute'?   *WOULDN'T KNOW. LEGGED IT (SEE ABOVE)*

Circumstances of Accident

Date of Accident: *8-5-2013*

Time of Accident: *2 p.m*

Precise Location of Accident: *KENNEALLY'S WINDOW*

Is there a White Line along the Centre of the Road?   Yes ☑   No ☐

Is it 'Broken' or 'Unbroken'?   *THE WINDOW IS BROKEN*

Describe the Weather: *CARDIGAN. BUTTONED.*

What was the Speed of your Vehicle:
(i) Prior to Accident (Miles Per Hour)?   *FIFTY*

(ii) At the Time of Impact (Miles Per Hour)?   *NOUGHT*

What Side of the Road was your Vehicle on at Time of Impact?   *INSIDE (THE SHOP)*

Who in Your Opinion was Responsible for the Accident?   *ABBA*

Describe Fully how the Accident Occurred: _BUSTER AND DERMOT WERE DRIVING ORPHANS TO CHOIR PRACTICE. THE POP GROUP ABBA (FROM SWEDEN) CAME ON THE RADIO WITH A SONG THE ORPHANS WANTED TO HEAR. TRYING TO TURN UP THE VOLUME, BUSTER FOUND HE HAD ACCIDENTALLY DRIVEN THE CAR THROUGH THE WINDOW OF KENNEALLY'S PAWN SHOP AT HIGH SPEED, AS IF IN A RAM-RAID, BUT DEFINITELY NOT A RAM-RAID. THEN THE POLICE CAR WENT UP THEIR ARSE. THE ORPHANS WERE SHOCKED AND RAN AWAY. DERMOT AND BUSTER CHASED THEM. ASSUME ORPHANS RAN INTO THE RIVER AND DISAPPEARED OR WERE TEMPTED INTO A MOUNTAIN BY A PIED PIPER CHARACTER. THE ABBA SONG WAS 'FERNANDO'_

Sketch of Accident:

Please draw a rough sketch (with appropriate measurements) showing the position of the vehicles and persons and the direction in which they were moving.

I CAN'T DRAW CARS

Declaration

I/we declare that the above particulars are true to the best of my/our knowledge. I/we hereby expressly authorize the company, if they do so require, to forward this form and any subsequent statement I/we or the driver may make, to any solicitors appointed to act in relation to any claim, prosecution or proceedings arising out of this incident. I/we further authorize the company, and/or any solicitors so instructed, to deal with all matters arising from this incident at their discretion and without any obligation to consult with or to obtain consent from me/us and to make any admission in connection with the said claim(s), prosecution(s) or proceedings which they in their absolute discretion may consider desirable or in the interests of me/us and/or the company.

I/we understand that you may ask for information from other insurers to check the answers I/we have provided.

Signature of Insured: _DERMOT BROWN_ Date: _20-5-2013_

THE PHONE

So, as you can see, there's no need to be scared of paper, unless an industrial roll of it falls off a flatbed and you're asleep at the bottom of a slope.

But what do you do when someone official calls up and talks to you with their voice? Don't pass it to your husband, especially if he's dead. Face up to the challenge. You're the head of the feckin' house. They can talk to you.

> ## Remember: your phone, your rules.

They're the rude ones, inviting themselves into your home, for no bigger reason than you're five months late with payments on your subs for the Limited Edition Porcelain Royal Doulton Steamrollers of Ireland collection.

Get some practice on cold callers. You know, the feckers ringing you from halfway round the world and calling themselves William or something – even though it sounds like it's the first time they've ever said the letter W in their lives – and offering you cheaper insurance or gas or double glazing or a holiday or whatever they're hawking.

Don't think of them as a Pain In The Answerphone. Think of them as a chance to have a bit of fun, and practise your phone technique. There's always plenty to chat about. If you've got a plan.

🖊BE POSITIVE

CALLER: Hello, could I speak to Mrs Brown?

MRS BROWN: Yes.

CALLER: Is that Mrs Brown?

MRS BROWN: Yes.

CALLER: *My arse* Hello there, Mrs Brown. My name's (Paul) and I'm calling from Double-Glazed Gas Holiday Insurance.

MRS BROWN: Yes.

CALLER: Is this a good time to talk?

MRS BROWN: Yes.

CALLER: Thank you, Mrs Brown. I just wanted to let you know about a great deal we've got on gas holidays and double glazing insurance. It's only €39.99 a month.

MRS BROWN: Yes.

CALLER: Is this the kind of thing you might be interested in?

MRS BROWN: Yes.

CALLER: Great. Perhaps I could take a few personal details?

MRS BROWN: Yes.

CALLER: So, can you confirm your address for me?

MRS BROWN: Yes.

CALLER: Right.

MRS BROWN: Yes.

CALLER: What is it?

MRS BROWN: Yes.

CALLER: Mrs Brown?

MRS BROWN: Yes.

CALLER: What's your address, please?

MRS BROWN: Yes.

CALLER: Yes?

MRS BROWN: Yes.

CALLER: Are you only going to say yes?

MRS BROWN: Yes.

CALLER: I'm going to end this call now, Mrs Brown.

MRS BROWN: What? And after I agreed with everything you said? You little fecker.

Now, I've kept that up for an entire *Jeremy Kyle* show before. And you don't have to pay any attention. You just wait for the gaps. It's like faking an organism, only more fun.

📞 TELL HIM ALL YOUR NEWS

CALLER: Hello, could I speak to Mrs Brown?

MRS BROWN: You already are, son.

CALLER: Hello there, Mrs Brown. My name's Paul –

MRS BROWN: Paul! How the devil are you?

CALLER: I'm very well, thank you.

MRS BROWN: Good. Because you know there's a fierce vomiting bug going around, don't you? Winnie next door says her Sharon's got it shooting out of both ends. She's like a garden sprinkler that got attached to the wrong pipe.

CALLER: Yes – Mrs Brown?

MRS BROWN: I had it myself, a few months back. Dreadful, it was. I collapsed in the National Wax Museum. Woke up seeing stars, I tell you. Jack Nicholson. Tina Turner. Ronan Keating. Ha ha! You have to laugh.

CALLER: Yes. Now, I just wanted to –

MRS BROWN: Anyway, I'm glad you've rung, Paul, because – can I tell you a little something? – today is my lucky day. Oh yes. And I'm not just saying that because Fintan Haverty sold me a book of marked bingo cards, guaranteed to win, even though he did – no, I'll tell you why: I was sitting here this morning reading *It's a Break* or whatever that magazine's called – full of shite, it was, especially the story about the woman who was abducted by an alien who whisked her off to his planet for a steamy intergalactic affair – mind you, I could see why he might have: she'd have beaten E.T. in an E.T. lookalike competition – anyway, I was sitting here, and a single white feather floated in through the window. And you know what they say about white feathers, don't you?

CALLER: No.

MRS BROWN: Ah, shite. I can't remember myself. It's something to do with angels and haircuts. Anyway, the point is: it's good luck. And I thought, Agnes, I thought to myself – I didn't say it out loud – I might be a bit unhinged but my doors haven't fallen off yet – I thought, Agnes, today is your lucky day. Now my Redser used to say he could only tell if it was his lucky day by popping down the bookie's and sticking a few punts either way on anything longer than 8-1, but I can feel it in my water, I'm telling you – unless, of course, that's the urine infection that's going round. There's been a shocking lot of it lately. Annie McEvoy says it's like passing hot drawing pins – poor thing, she's walking like she's holding a goldfish bowl between her knees. Three buses pass her before she gets to the bus stop. And it's only at the end of her path . . .

This one takes more effort, I'll grant you. But it's all worth it just to hear the little creep squirming on the other end of the line. One of them put his line manager on once. Then his office manager. If I'd stayed on there another hour, I reckon I could have had a one-to-one with the King of India.

PLAN 3:

FRIGHTEN THE SHITE OUT OF HIM

CALLER: Hello, could I speak to Mrs Brown?

MRS BROWN: This is she.

CALLER: Hello there, Mrs Brown. My name's Paul and I'm calling from Double Holidays Gas Glazing Insurance.

MRS BROWN: Ssh!

CALLER: What?

MRS BROWN: Can you hear that?

CALLER: Hear what?

MRS BROWN: Never mind. It was probably nothing.

CALLER: As I say, my name's Paul, and –

MRS BROWN: There it is again!

CALLER: What?

MRS BROWN: The noise. It sounded like someone forcing a window open.

CALLER: Oh. Can you see anything?

MRS BROWN: Of course I can't. There's been a power cut.

CALLER: Right. Well –

MRS BROWN: Ssh! There's someone in the kitchen.

CALLER: Are you expecting anybody?

MRS BROWN: Are you mad? The whole town's in lockdown.

CALLER: Lockdown?

MRS BROWN: Don't you read the papers, Paul? The Beast of Dublin is on the prowl.

CALLER: The Beast of –?

MRS BROWN: Ssh! He's coming up the stairs!

CALLER: I think I'd better hang up, Mrs Brown, so you can call the police.

MRS BROWN: No, Paul. It's too late for that now. Stay with me. Don't leave me alone. Please. DON'T LEAVE ME ALONE TO DIE, PAUL!

CALLER: Give me your address, quickly. I'll get one of my colleagues to call the police.

MRS BROWN: I'm not giving my address out to a total stranger. I might be in mortal peril, but I'm no fool. Besides, how do I know it's not you coming across the landing, opening the door. – and –

Open the squeakiest cupboard in the house
AAAARRRGGGGHHHHHH!

Now slam the door shut and go SILENT

CALLER: Mrs Brown? Mrs Brown . . . ?

MRS BROWN: Ah. It was just our Dermot. Drunk again. Little shite.

Believe me, after this one, they never call back.

THE EMPTY NEST

It happens to all of us, if you're lucky to live long enough to see it.

For years you've been at their beck and call, never a moment to yourself, running, fetching, washing, picking up, a shoulder to cry on, a strong back to lift them, a pair of caring hands to wipe their arse ...

And then, before you know it ... they're gone.

They're married. They're having kids of their own. Or they're on the Lord's work in Africa, bringing the Bible to the little Chinese children. Or they're a ship's cobbler on board an icebreaker or whatever it was I told people Dermot was doing when he was in prison. For the life of me I can't remember. It changed every day. I was driven spare with the feckin' shame of it, it's a wonder I could remember my own name, let alone keep a story straight down the Co-Op.

Anyway, they're gone.

For a day or two, you're kicking your heels, eating a whole pack of Marie Thins to yourself. Living the dream. Then it hits you.

The feckin' silence.

Your own home – a place that was always filled with noise and laughter – is quiet. No one to talk to, except Grandad and the dog. And a woman needs proper conversation, not all that slavering and growling. No wonder I end up talking to the feckin' dog.

Sure, you want your children to move on. It's the sign you've done your job properly.

A child that's strong enough to fly the nest is a living testament to a Mammy's love. What else are we here for? From the moment they slip out from between your legs, they're after leaving you. The long goodbye, they call it. And yet it can feel like you've hardly said hello before they're packing their stuff in bin bags and leaving another room empty.

I sometimes think how it would be if Redser were still alive, if it were just the two of us. Me and him, finally having all that time together that we never had because of the kids. That's what I call a lucky feckin' escape right there.

So there you are. On your own except the tick of the clock and Grandad, snoring in his armchair.

You've put out some tinned marrowbone chunks, a bowl of water, and maybe something for the dog.

What the feck do you do now?

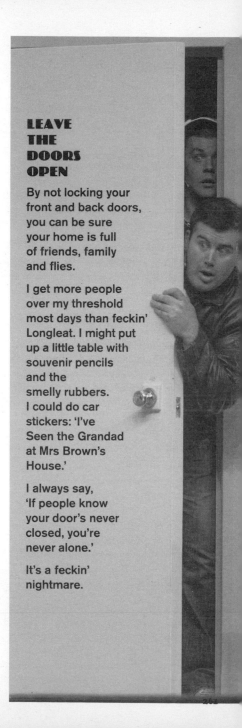

LEAVE THE DOORS OPEN

By not locking your front and back doors, you can be sure your home is full of friends, family and flies.

I get more people over my threshold most days than feckin' Longleat. I might put up a little table with souvenir pencils and the smelly rubbers. I could do car stickers: 'I've Seen the Grandad at Mrs Brown's House.'

I always say, 'If people know your door's never closed, you're never alone.'

It's a feckin' nightmare.

SALESPEOPLE AT THE DOOR

'Have you considered changing your gas supplier?' Ah, the sweetest sound you can hear. I could go on for hours, nattering to one of these wee doorstep hawkers in their cheap suits. To be honest, the amount of static coming off most of these chisellers' suits, you wouldn't need to pay for electricity, just wire them up to your lights direct.

But God love them, don't leave them on the doorstep. Invite them in. Talk about the weather. Find out what they think about the Stiffy On The Liffey. Get them to have a look at that rash that's worrying you.

If they're roughly the size of one of your lot, you can get them to try on any second-hand clothes you've bought. *'What size are you, darling? 34C? Try on this bra for my Cathy, would you?'* *'You're the shape of my Mark. Can I see what you look like in this frogman's outfit?'* That sort of thing.

> **!** **Remember:** they're trained to not be the one who stops the conversation. They're meant to keep you talking. They don't know they're dealing with a feckin' professional.

Just don't sign anything. Say you need to discuss it with your husband. They don't know he's in an urn on the fucking sideboard. I imagine he was perfectly happy with his last gas supplier, God rest his soul, unless these feckers want to outbid the crematorium.

GODBOTHERERS

Gas and electric salesmen are not bad, but the cream de la cream are the Godbotherers. The Jehoover's Witnesses. The Church of the Saturday Saints. Ah, the Good Lord loves a trier.

My door is always open to the Lord. It's open to everybody. I must get Mark to have a go at the snib with his WD40.

But if it's been a long day and *Quincy*'s not on for hours, sometimes one of them door-to-door evangelistas can be a feckin' godsend.

I invite them in, make them a cup of tea whether they want one or not, and we have a proper good chinwag about the Bible. I love it. I won a prize at school for Bible Study. 'Most Likely to be Burnt at the Feckin' Stake'. They don't know who they're dealing with.

My record is four and a half hours and a half-gallon of tea. I had to send Winnie out for more teabags.

In the end, the lad ran off, claiming he had seen a burning bush in the garden. He thought it was a miracle. I've told Dermot not to flick his butts out the upstairs window during a dry spell.

Anyway, here are some Bible stories you might want to discuss, and some questions you can ask your guest, to keep the conversation flowing.

NOAH'S ARK

The Lord is raging because mankind's so wicked, so he sends forty days and nights of rain as a punishment. (Round our way, a spell that short wouldn't be a curse, it'd be a feckin' blessing.) He tells Noah to build himself a boat and take two of every animal in the world except dinosaurs, and wait it out.

1. Did Noah sail round the world first to get all the animals? That'd be an amazing adventure right there. Why did you leave that bit out? This might be the word of God, but your man has no feckin' idea how to tell a story.

2. We had two feckin' hamsters and I was never through cleaning the shite out of the sawdust. Why didn't the Ark sink under the weight of it all? That'd be how to prove the story was true. Send your lads from *Time Team* out looking for evidence of a terrible shitwreck.

3. What about the fishes and the sharks and the whales? Sure, there's no point putting them on a boat when they can swim alongside the feckin' thing. So did he tether them? Or catch them? How big were his nets? They must have been the size of feckin' circus tents.

4. What the feck had the dinosaurs done wrong? Seems awful harsh to wipe them out because man's bollixed things up. And what about the dinosaurs that can swim? You can't drown them. Is that how we've still got the Loch Ness Monster? What happened to the second Loch Ness Monster? Did he get eaten by one of the sharks? Let me freshen that cup.

JONAH AND THE WHALE

Jonah gets on the Lord's bad side, which is not a good idea, and he's on a ship when a fierce storm blows up, so he says 'throw me overboard', and the sailors do, and he's only eaten by a whale. Three days later he comes out of the whale, stinking of fish, and goes to find Geppetto who tells him he can be a real boy.

1. Hasn't your whale got a big fence in his mouth? I'm sure I saw that on the TV. How did Jonah fit through? I was a slip of a thing when I was young, and I had trouble climbing through Redser's parents' kitchen window of a night. Was he one of them anorectics? Is that how he didn't need to eat in there?

2. Three days? What was he doing in there? No. Don't tell me. I've raised enough boys. I know what he was up to. In the dark. Thinking nobody was watching. Talk about a feckin' sperm whale.

3. Hang on. It's not Geppetto. It's Jiminy Cricket.

ST PAUL ON THE ROAD TO DOMESTOS

Some fella called Saul is knocked over by a bright light, hears the voice of God, goes blind for three days and changes his name to Paul. He writes a book of the Bible and gets his own cathedral.

1. You call that a feckin' miracle? The same thing happened to my Redser all the time. Well, he kept being knocked down by a bright light on the front of the 31 bus, going blind and forgetting his name. I had to stop him going down Foley's with the chequebook. Can I tempt you to a biscuit? I've only broken ones left but it all goes down the same hole.

HE'S EVEN APPEARING ON THE FECKIN' TOAST

ABRAHAM AND ISAAC

The Lord tells Abraham to sacrifice his son Isaac, and Abraham ties the lad up and comes at him with a sword, and then God sends an angel to tell him not to do it, saying he's proved his faith.

1. Well, he's proved something. He's proved he's a feckin' psychopath. If there's a shop that'll do a mug with 'Worst Dad Ever' on it, I know what Isaac's getting Abraham for feckin' Christmas. Sure, you want to murder the little bollixes sometimes, but there's taking things too far. Where were Social Services?

2. God's pretty down on killing when he dishes out the Ten Commandments, but here he's like Hannibal feckin' Lecter. Did he change his mind? Does he do that? Is he going to change his mind about adultery? Because Kathleen O'Riordan down the bingo'd be feckin' delighted to hear she might have a loophole.

MAKE TOAST

If you've run out of salesmen and Godbotherers, there's always toast to be made. And the smell of toast draws a family in like a feckin' lighthouse. Make yourself a slice, you'll never feckin' eat it. 'Ah, you got toast on?' and there they are. Swiping it from your side plate like a swarm of locusts. I reckon if I was lost in the feckin' Gobi Desert with only a loaf of bread, I could be found and rescued by the kids in about thirty seconds by laying a couple of slices out to toast in the sun. It's like sending up a feckin' flare. You're never alone with toast.

CROSSWORDS

I do love a crossword. I tried one of them Scoobydookoos, but I couldn't get any of the words to fit.

You're never alone with a crossword. Probably because some fecker's always leaning over your shoulder trying to tell you what Four Across is.

But doing a crossword keeps the brain active and it fills up a good chunk of the day. I like to think of it as a battle of wits. Me, doing my crossword, versus Grandad trying to interrupt me because he's got his head caught in the feckin' catflap again.

Some crosswords are harder than others, so you might need a helping hand. Here are some of the trickiest clues I've ever solved. If these come up again, you've got a head start.

Constipation (9 letters) = **NNNNNNNNN**

Religious garment (11) = **NUNDERPANTS**

Pet lover (8) = **CATHOLIC**

Burden (7) = **GRANDAD**

Fishing technique (8) = **CASTANET**

Plate-shaped (7) = **SORCERY**

Amusing novelty hat (8) = **SILICONE**

Waste disposal unit (7) = **GRANDAD**

The root of all evil (5) = **PENIS**

Contraceptive (8) = **STOPCOCK**

Dish made with eggs and pork (6) = **HAMLET**

Prehistoric creature (7) = **GRANDAD**

Jobless (8) = **WOODWORK**

Overall (7) = **WORKTOP**

Pertaining to food storage (6) = **FRIGID**

Unhygienic (7) = **GRANDAD**

Discreet gesture (9) = **MICROWAVE**

Statesman (8) = **GOBSHITE**

Like a cemetery (5) = **GRAVY**

Household pest (7) = **GRANDAD**

Measure of acidity (9) = **LIMESCALE**

To search without success (7) = **MANHUNT**

Fiancé using neck (anag) (7,8) = **FECKIN' NUISANCE**

Mammy's Tip

Deal with the problem of stubborn toilet stains by making Grandad do his sit-downs in the pub.

I am proud to say that I have never once left a crossword unfinished. I know some people use a pencil, but I like a pen. It shows confidence. If some of the letters turn out to be wrong, if a word doesn't fit, you can always go back and write over the top.

To show you what you can do if you put your mind to it, here's one I finished. It's from the back of a Watchtower *(the Jehoovers Witnesses left it behind when they had to dash off – apparently they'd left the iron on).*

If the crossword's too much for your head, try a wordsearch. The answers are all already there. You've just got to find them. You know the things – they always come in those magazines with a slut on the front. Sure, I've never known why. Perhaps it's to fool the old giffers into buying them, making them think it's a mucky book.

Here's one I did in a hurry on the bus. I might not have found all the words.

Keep going, and eventually you can leave a crossword on the kitchen table that will make everyone think, 'That woman, she's more than meets the eye.'

23. The Beauty of nature

the countryside is resplendent in her simple glory. see how many words you can find from the list below

RAINBOW	WILLOW	PEACH
LILAC	BEE	FRAGRANT
FLUFFY	FRESH	LOCH
MEADOW	CLOUD	OAK
FLEECE	BUDS	MIST
RAGWEED	FOREST	TRUFFLE
BEAUTY	DRAKE	TEAL

DUSTING

The important thing is to look busy. When the family drop round, you have to look like you're ready to drop yourself. 'The work is never done', that's the impression you want to give.

If they know you've been sitting with your feet up all day watching *Homes Under the Hammer* and doing the word snake in the back of the paper, they'll be filling your day with their bollocks and then you've no time for telly-shopping.

First things first: everything needs dusting. It's not heavy work, but it fills the day.

When you've got little ones, dusting is easily forgotten: you've not got the time. When I had the twins, I had shelves that were so thick with dust it looked like I was storing a fur coat up there. I had a knick-knack cabinet fall off the wall with the weight of it.

But now you've got the time, crack out the duster.

I read in a magazine somewhere that dust is human skin, so I reckon in the average year, in an averagely filthy house, without even knowing it, you've probably eaten a whole person. That's cannibalism, and I can't condone that.

I copied this out of an article by some rubber-gloved gobshite off the telly who makes a living bossing people about, and she said there are places that people forget to dust. I've added a few of my own, and I say if you can include these in your dusting routine, you can probably kill most of a day.

Places people forget to dust

pelmets

curtain rails

underneath ornaments

the top of the can of Pledge

the inside of clocks

under the doormat

Grandad's head

bathplugs

flowers

the 'special occasion' section of your knicker drawer

Dermot's dirty magazine stash (damp cloth and rubber gloves)

the underside of doors

between the panels of radiators

the tins in your cupboards

the drum of the washing machine

all that stuff on top of your kitchen cupboards you never use (yoghurt maker, Sodastream, box of electric feckin' spaghetti forks)

the fusebox

the breadbin

the roof

Not that I get time, with people dropping in all hours of the day and night because I've left my door open. You see – it all adds up.

Always dust with a proper duster *(or old pair of underpants)* and furniture polish. Don't be tempted to use the hoover.

I had this beautiful china model of his Holiness we'd picked up at Lourdes, and didn't the feckin' thing go up the tube. I rearranged the ornaments on the shelf and never mentioned it to Redser till the day he died. I don't know why, but I couldn't bring myself to tell him I'd sucked off the Pope.

ORGANIZING YOUR PILLS

When a woman approaches middle age, like me, she needs a helping hand with those little niggles and twinges, and it's down to Dr Flynn for a pick-me-up. Pretty soon, just organizing your pills can be a full-time job.

I'm lucky. I've got my health. I mean, I get the odd ache and pain, mainly in my knees. I blame all that praying. But, as I always say, when the big feller wants you down on your knees, putting your lips to good use in his service, you put up with a bit of discomfort. But by and large, I'm in good shape.

I have these little pills to take for arthritis – glucosameanie or something – but they're easy enough to swallow with a cup of tea. Sure they're big. I have to feckin' dunk them. But it's not like I'm a martyr to tablets, unlike some people I know. I don't want to name any names, but here's a picture of Winnie.

But even Winnie's nothing compared to Kathleen O'Murtagh. Now, even if you'd never met her, you'd know her a mile off, because with all the pills she has to take, she must sound like a pair of feckin' maracas coming down the street.

She's got blood pressure tablets, water tablets, thyroid tablets, heart tablets, rheumatism tablets, arthritis tablets, tablets to stop her hot flushes, tablets to stop her cold feet – it's a wonder she's ever the right temperature. She's like the porridge in that story about the three feckin' bears. Jaysus, if she's not a walking miracle, I don't know what is. It's only the tablets keeping her in one piece.

(That reminds me. Father Quinn once told me he'd such a knowledge of the Bible he reckoned he could find a passage on any subject you cared to name. Any subject at all. I said, Father, you're on. And come Mass one Sunday, I slipped a little bit of folded-up paper into his hand. He got to the pulpit and unfolded it. And his face went pale when he saw what I'd written: CONSTIPATION. But God love him, he opened the Good Book, cleared his throat and started to read. 'And Moses . . . took the tablets . . .')

The way to keep on top of your pills is to do what Kathleen does with hers: buy one of those boxes with the little days of the week compartments in it. Every Sunday, she sits down and dishes out dozens of pills. It's a ritual for her. Right between Mass and Sunday roast. That's her Sunday: Mass, pills, roast, would you believe?

It's a good job I was round there when the string on her rosary broke. Half the beads ended up in her pill box. And with her wonky eyesight, I wouldn't have trusted her not to choke on one of the damn things.

Once you've got your pills organized, you can join the competitive sport of Who's Got The Most Pills? I swear, with most mammies, their age is the same as the percentage of their conversation taken up with comparing feckin' tablets. 'Have you got these yellow ones, Iris?' 'Ah, sure, I've got three different sorts of yellow ones. Have you got the blue ones with the tiny writing on them?' 'Course I have. And the blue and white ones. Oh, and the little diamond-shaped ones that taste like soap. They're all the rage now. You haven't got those, so?' It's like that 'I went shopping and I bought a . . .' game.

And when their hubbies pass away, there's the Mammy's ritual of putting all his bottles of pills in a big feckin' shopping bag and returning them to the pharmacist. Like a votive offering. When my Redser died, I did a similar thing and took all his empties back to the pub. I think some of them ended up in a museum.

AH, JUST ONE MORE BEFORE YOU GO

We might as well finish the pot.

What else do you need to know? Maybe I've told you enough. Anyone who knows me knows that I'm not really one for too much talking.

I could say more. I've barely touched on window ledges, or colic, and I've some pretty strong opinions on crazy paving. But it's only advice. And, despite everything I've said, you have to remember there are no hard and fast rules.

Like so many things in life – love, work, motherhood, that dodgy Taiwanese sat-nav Buster gave Dermot for his birthday – the best idea sometimes is to stop listening and find your own way.

I can talk it up all I like, as if I know the answers because I've got a half-dozen or so great children, and a handful of beautiful grandchildren, kids who I sometimes think must have been sent by the feckin' angels, they're so deep down perfect.

But then I think, 'How did I get here?' And the answer is: guesswork and good luck. Again, like Dermot's sat-nav.

When I first started running my own home, I didn't know what I was doing. I was nothing but a girl. I didn't have any qualifications. They say there's no exam to pass to be a Mammy, and even if there was, I'd only have bollixed the theory and aced the oral.

The honest truth is you have to take yourself in hand, pick yourself up by the scruff of the neck, put your back into it and chance your arm – it might take a bit of legwork to keep your shoulder to the wheel, but if you go with your gut, grit your teeth, knuckle down and give it plenty of elbow grease, keep your chin up and your hair on, and throw yourself in head first with both feet, then fingers crossed you won't go arse over tit.

It really is that simple.

Being a Mammy is the hardest job in the world, but if you do it long enough, you find out the secret.

You may not get a €1,000,000 paycheck and a six-figure bonus, like some flash lad in banking; you may not get the respect of your community, like a doctor or a teacher; you may not get fame and glory, like a pop star or a footballer, but you do get something.

If you find out what it is, drop me a line.

Now feck off. I've got a family to look after.

For my birthday, the boys came round and performed highlights from Cornetto.

BIBLIOGRAPHY

They told me you always put one
of these bibble-bibble-whatsits
at the end of a book. They said:
'Make a list of all the texts you
consulted while you were writing
yours, Mrs Brown.' Well, it's a bit
late for that now. I've finished.
I mean, I looked in my address
book a few times. I remember
checking a couple of spellings with
the *Yellow Pages*. And I definitely
polished off a couple of Puzzlers.
But otherwise, how the feck should
I remember?

So, just to make sure I haven't
missed anything, here's a list
of all the books on my shelves.
They're mainly romantic novels,
but what's wrong with that?
We can't all be literary. I've never
read anything by Harry Potter, and
I don't suppose I ever will. But I
know what I like, and that's a bit of
fantasy. (And by that, I mean a big
strong man sweeping a girl off her
feet, not a list of feckin' dragons
and a map of an unpronounceable
place that would wipe the floor in
Scrabble.) If you've spent all day
tied to the sink in rubber gloves,
you want a bit of good, honest
escapism. And these do the job
just grand.

Mammy's Tip
Avoid dampness in clothes by
not borrowing Winnie's copy of
Fifty Shades of Grey.

- *A Convenient Millionaire* – Leonardella Grey
- *They Couldn't Tame the Postmistress* – Jennifer Kettle
- *Wheelbarrow of Love* – Penny Hamn
- *The Enormous Husband* – Meg Trowell
- *Betty, Savage Empress of the Plains* – Satsuma Dennis
- *A Devil on the Top Deck* – Nanette Roast
- *Midnight Welshman* – Susan Wind
- *A Powerful Hairdresser* – Primula Cobb
- *Unexpected Heart in Bagging Area* – Hilda Wellish
- *The Notorious Honeymoon* – Sarah Flan
- *Bernard: Man of Destiny* – Rita Kojak
- *The Corduroy Phantom* – Nerys Bunk
- *The Officer and the Doctor and the Forbidden Bride to Remember* – Nester Champion
- *He Stole her Slippers* – C. R. Shelf
- *Yesterday's Plumber* – Angela Sister
- *Malcolmio: Romany Tycoon* – Louise O'Botillioni
- *The Reluctant Headmaster* – Camilla Fletch
- *Love Robot 2-X* – J. T. T. 'Prof' Benz
- *Reining the Duty Manager* – Lin Jars
- *Princess Pam* – Isabelle Wall
- *The Captain's Cough* – P. Harriet Wealth
- *Mask of the Forbidden Bassoonist* – Karen Plant
- *He Never Fixed the Fridge* – Lindana Ragu
- *Lord Fondlebottom's Secret* – Helen Dish
- *A Cowboy for Christmas* – Val Weather
- *The All-Night Garage Grille Cannot Sunder Us* – Tina Nimmo
- *A Whisper in Her Stockings* – Justine Radish
- *The Enchanted Handyman* – Olivia Lunch
- *Cinderella's Substance* – Margaret Shoes
- *The Hellion and the Fishmonger* – Pat Winsome
- *Part-Time Gypsy* – Daniella Wainscotting
- *Lovestruck in the Loft* – Hope Grain
- *The Highwayman's Code* – H. M. S. Office
- *The Tender Tea Lady* – Henrietta Cruttsniff
- *Three Times a Bailiff* – Jean Chairs
- *Bathroom of Destiny* – Bev Plank
- *The Unwilling Sewage Worker* – Diane Yessing
- *Surrender to My Arms, Miriam* – Trina St Frutiger
- *Your Heart, Milady* – Dr G. P. Edgebaston
- *The Secret Man* – Ann Lady
- *An Unexpected Fist* – Fiona Hapless
- *A Kiss by the Sluice* – Wendy Gist
- *The Princess and the Pizza* – Felicity Tunnel
- *Beekeepers by Night* – Lydia Hand
- *From Roy with Love* – Stephanie Muller-Rice
- *The Scent of Aeroplane Glue* – Clive Bunk
- *Mistletoe Chiropodist* – Maz Pots
- *The Forbidden Potato Man* – Joanna Napkin
- *Shed of Pleasure* – Kim Louvre
- *The Impatient Surgeon* – Barbara Barham Abraham
- *Dormobile of Destiny* – Chris Thumb
- *Runaway Binman* – Bev Toucan
- *Moonlit Subcommittee* – Ingrid Kohlrabi
- *Who Can Deny the Dentist?* – Ursula Cloybeam
- *Slave to the Tea Trolley* – Alison Dosshouse
- *The Duffle Coat Lies Untoggled* – Carla Tea
- *Supply Teachers Don't Care* – Kirsty Gunwale
- *An Uninvited Tramp* – Fran Head
- *Buccaneer of the Laundromat* – Holly Modem
- *A Kiss from the Returning Officer* – Peggy Saucer
- *Love's Policeman* – Ryvita Olaf
- *A Perfect Clown* – Pippa Earworm
- *Love in the Shoe Bins* – T. D. Stadt
- *Forever, Graham* – Lilette Dust
- *The Wonderful Rotarian* – Julie Hand
- *Unchain the Nightwatchman* – Molly Jeep
- *The Jumble Sale Texan* – Rosemary Pith
- *The Milkman Prince* – Maureen Owls
- *Re-heeled with Love* – P. F. Lap
- *Chain Ferry of Hearts* – Eleanor Vange
- *You Will Meet a Tall, Dark Lollipop-man* – Gilda Chips
- *The Undermanager's Revenge* – Ribena House
- *Janet and the Alderman* – Janet Alderman

ACKNOWLEDGEMENTS

There's plenty of people to thank who helped me get this book into shape.

First off, my family. Without them, I'd have had peace and quiet, plenty of time to put pen to paper, a nice clear head – and fuck all to write about.

Then there's my friends: Winnie, Mr Foley, Fathers Quinn and Damian. Fine and good people, to a man. In Winnie's case, to several men.

Then there's Billy at the newsagent. Without him, I'd have had to pay full whack for a box of pens and a feckin' great notebook. He did me a lovely discount.

I'd like to thank Mac from the bookies for keeping his big mouth shut about me getting the money to write a book – *but I can't* because the scuttering gobshite told *every* fecker who wafted in off the street. If I had a penny for *every* time I've had my feckin' ear bent in two by some goon with a *'nice little filly in the 3.25 at Limerick'* I'd have a damn sight more than if I'd backed any one of the feckin' nags I was being feckin' nagged to go halves on.

A few other thanks to people who persuaded me to mention them: Pat Mulligan, who said he'd give me €10; Molly Savage, who said

I could have her posh hairdryer with the big colander thing on the end; Shammy McGinty, who's now doing my windows for free for a year; and Mickey Quinn, who's going to let me off the last four payments for that inflatable Christ I still haven't found a use for.

And last, but not least, I must say a big thank you to Ginger Pubes at Penguin. A fine lad, although he should never have dyed his hair.

Oh, and thanks to me, without whom this book would have been either a lot shorter or about something else.

Special thank you to Daniel Bunyard at Penguin Publishing